Careers in Focus

JOURNALISM

SECOND EDITION

Ferguson's

An Infobase Learning Company

Careers in Focus: Journalism

Ferguson's
An imprint of Infobase Learning
132 West 31st Street
New York NY 10001

Library of Congress Cataloging-in-Publication Data

Careers in focus : Journalism. — 2nd ed.
    p. cm.
  Includes bibliographical references and index.
  ISBN-13: 978-0-8160-8031-1 (hardcover : alk. paper)
  ISBN-10: 0-8160-8031-3 (hardcover : alk. paper) 1. Journalism—Juvenile
literature. 2. Journalism—Vocational guidance—Juvenile literature. I. J.G.
Ferguson Publishing Company. II. Title: Journalism.
  PN4776.C35 2011
  070.5023—dc22

                                                          2010046353

Ferguson's books are available at special discounts when purchased in bulk
quantities for businesses, associations, institutions, or sales promotions.
Please call our Special Sales Department in New York at (212) 9670-8800 or
(800) 322-8755.

You can find Ferguson's on the World Wide Web at
http://www.infobaselearning.com

Text design by David Strelecky
Composition by Newgen North America
Cover printed by Yurchak Printing, Landisville, Pa.
Book printed and bound by Yurchak Printing, Landisville, Pa.
Date printed: April 2011
Printed in the United States of America

10 9 8 7 6 5 4 3 2 1

This book is printed on acid-free paper.

All links and Web addresses were checked and verified to be correct at the time
of publication. Because of the dynamic nature of the Web, some addresses and
links may have changed since publication and may no longer be valid.

Table of Contents

Introduction

Careers in Focus: Journalism describes a variety of careers in the deadline-driven, yet rewarding, world of journalism—at newspapers, magazines, publishing companies, and radio and television stations, and on the Internet. These careers are as diverse in nature as they are in their earnings and educational requirements. Earnings range from minimum wage or less for editorial and research assistants to more than $1 million for top network news anchors. A few of these careers—such as editorial and research assistants—require a few years of postsecondary education, but are excellent starting points for a career in the industry. Other technically oriented jobs, such as printing press operators and assistants, require some postsecondary training and on-the-job training. Many positions in this industry (such as art directors, editors, reporters, and writers) require a minimum of a bachelor's degree. Journalism professors at four-year colleges and universities need at least a master's degree.

The outlook for journalism jobs is expected to be keenly competitive in the coming years. In fact, the *Career Guide to Industries* predicts that employment in the newspaper, magazine, and book publishing industries will decline by 19 percent through 2018. Employment in journalistic broadcasting is expected to increase by 7 percent through 2018—slower than the 11 percent growth expected for all industries.

Despite these predictions, the field of journalism plays a major role in our lives. Journalists and support workers are responsible for providing timely and sometimes urgent information to the public. Also, more and more print and broadcast entities are producing electronic versions (on the Web, smartphones, etc.), which will require reporters, editors, photographers, videographers, writers, producers, and graphic artists with specialized training and skill in creating content for electronic publication. Opportunities will be especially strong for workers who have advanced education and knowledge of the latest technology.

Each article in *Careers in Focus: Journalism* discusses a particular occupation in detail. The articles appear in Ferguson's *Encyclopedia of Careers and Vocational Guidance*, but they have been updated and revised with the latest information from the U.S. Department of Labor, professional organizations, and other sources.

The **Quick Facts** section provides a brief summary of the career, including recommended school subjects, personal skills, work environment, minimum educational requirements, salary ranges, certification or licensing requirements, and employment outlook. This section also provides acronyms and identification numbers for the following government classification indexes: the Dictionary of Occupational Titles (DOT), the Guide for Occupational Exploration (GOE), the National Occupational Classification (NOC) Index, and the Occupational Information Network (O*NET)-Standard Occupational Classification System (SOC) index. The DOT, GOE, and O*NET-SOC indexes have been created by the U.S. government; the NOC index is Canada's career classification system. Readers can use the identification numbers listed in the Quick Facts section to access further information about a career. Print editions of the DOT (*Dictionary of Occupational Titles*. Indianapolis, Ind.: JIST Works, 1991) and GOE (*Guide for Occupational Exploration*. Indianapolis, Ind.: JIST Works, 2001) are available at libraries. Electronic versions of the DOT (http://www.oalj.dol.gov/libdot.htm), NOC (http://www5.hrsdc.gc.ca/NOC), and O*NET-SOC (http://online.onetcenter.org) are available on the Internet. When no DOT, GOE, NOC, or O*NET-SOC numbers are listed, this means that the U.S. Department of Labor or Human Resources and Skills Development Canada have not created a numerical designation for this career. In this instance, you will see the acronym "N/A," or not available.

The **Overview** section is a brief introductory description of the duties and responsibilities involved in this career. Oftentimes, a career may have a variety of job titles. When this is the case, alternative career titles are presented. Employment statistics are also provided, when available. The **History** section describes the history of the particular job as it relates to the overall development of its industry or field. **The Job** describes the primary and secondary duties of the job. **Requirements** discusses high school and postsecondary education and training requirements, any certification or licensing that is necessary, and other personal requirements for success in the job. **Exploring** offers suggestions on how to gain experience in or knowledge of the particular job before making a firm educational and financial commitment. The focus is on what can be done while still in high school (or in the early years of college) to gain a better understanding of the job. The **Employers** section gives an overview of typical places of employment for the job. **Starting Out** discusses the best ways to land that first job, be it through the college career services office, newspaper ads, Internet employment sites, or personal contact. The **Advancement** section describes what kind of career path to expect from the job and how to get there. **Earnings** lists salary ranges and describes the typical fringe benefits. The **Work**

Environment section describes the typical surroundings and conditions of employment—whether indoors or outdoors, noisy or quiet, social or independent. Also discussed are typical hours worked, any seasonal fluctuations, and the stresses and strains of the job. The **Outlook** section summarizes the job in terms of the general economy and industry projections. For the most part, Outlook information is obtained from the U.S. Bureau of Labor Statistics and is supplemented by information gathered from professional associations. Job growth terms follow those used in the *Occupational Outlook Handbook*. Growth described as "much faster than the average" means an increase of 20 percent or more. Growth described as "faster than the average" means an increase of 14 to 19 percent. Growth described as "about as fast as the average" means an increase of 7 to 13 percent. Growth described as "more slowly than the average" means an increase of 3 to 6 percent. "Little or no change" means a decrease of 2 percent to an increase of 2 percent. "Decline" means a decrease of 3 percent or more. Each article ends with **For More Information**, which lists organizations that provide information on training, education, internships, scholarships, and job placement.

Careers in Focus: Journalism also includes photos, informative sidebars, and interviews with professionals in the field.

Whether you are interested in art, current events, fashion, photography, or politics, there is a chance for you to have a rewarding career in the field of journalism. Read about the different opportunities available, and be sure to contact the organizations listed for more information. Good luck with your career exploration!

Art Directors

QUICK FACTS

School Subjects
Art
Computer science
Journalism

Personal Skills
Artistic
Communication/ideas

Work Environment
Primarily indoors
Primarily one location

Minimum Education Level
Bachelor's degree

Salary Range
$41,670 to $78,580 to
$160,060+

Certification or Licensing
None available

Outlook
About as fast as the average

DOT
164

GOE
01.01.01

NOC
5131

O*NET-SOC
27-1011.00

OVERVIEW

In journalistic publishing, *art directors* work with artists, photographers, illustrators, desktop publishing specialists, and text and photo editors to develop visual images and generate copy. They are responsible for evaluating existing illustrations and photographs, choosing new illustrations and photographs, determining presentation styles and techniques, hiring both staff and freelance talent, working with layouts, and preparing budgets.

Art directors are also employed by advertising agencies to oversee the creation of an advertisement or ad campaign, television commercials, posters, and packaging, as well as in film and video and on the Internet.

In sum, art directors are charged with informing and educating consumers. They supervise both in-house and off-site staff, handle executive issues, and oversee the entire artistic production process. There are approximately 84,200 art directors working in the United States.

HISTORY

The first art directors were probably staff illustrators for book publishers. As the publishing industry grew more complex and incorporated new technologies such as photography and film, art direction evolved into a more supervisory position and became a full-time job. Publishers and advertisers began to need specialists who could acquire and use illustrations and photos. Women's magazines such as *Vogue* (http://www.vogue.com) and *Harper's Bazaar* (http://www.harpersbazaar.com), and photo magazines, such as *National Geographic* (http://www.nationalgeographic.com), relied so much on illustration and photography that the photo editor and art director began to carry as much power as the text editor.

Today's art directors supervise almost every type of visual project produced. Through a variety of methods and media, from magazines and newspapers to film and television, comic books, and the Internet, art directors communicate ideas by selecting and supervising every element that goes into the finished product.

THE JOB

Art directors are responsible for all visual aspects of printed or on-screen projects. Art directors, even those with specialized backgrounds, must be skilled in and knowledgeable about design, illustration, photography, computers, research, and writing in order to supervise the work of graphic artists, photographers, illustrators, desktop publishing specialists, text and photo editors, and other employees.

In publishing, art directors may begin with the editorial department's concept or develop one in collaboration with these and other publishing professionals. Once the concept is established, art directors need to decide on the most effective way to communicate it by asking a variety of questions. What is the overall tone of the publication? (Serious? Thought-provoking? Comedic?) How will the illustrations complement the text? If only a small amount of text is being used, how will the illustrations be used to communicate information to the reader? What type of format (print, online, or both) will be used? Additionally, if an article or feature is being revised, existing illustrations must be reevaluated.

After deciding what needs to be illustrated, art directors must find sources that can create or provide the art. Photo agencies, for example, have photographs and illustrations on thousands of different subjects. If, however, the desired illustration does not exist, it may have to be commissioned or designed by one of the staff designers or illustrators. Commissioning artwork means that the art director contacts a photographer or illustrator and explains what is needed. A price is negotiated, and the artist creates the image specifically for the art director.

Once the illustrations and other art elements have been secured, they must be presented in an appealing manner. The art director supervises (and may help in the production of) the layout of the piece and presents the final version to the editorial director. Laying out is the process of figuring out where every image, headline, and block of text will be placed on the page. The size, style, and method of reproduction must all be specifically indicated so that the image is re-created as the director intended it.

Technology has been playing an increasingly important role in the art director's job. Most art directors, for example, use a variety of computer software programs, including Adobe InDesign, FrameMaker, Illustrator, Photoshop, QuarkXPress, and CorelDRAW. Many others create and oversee Web sites for publishers and work with other interactive media and materials, including CD-ROM, touch screens, multidimensional visuals, and new animation programs.

Art directors usually work on more than one project at a time and must be able to keep numerous, unrelated details straight. They often work under pressure of a deadline and yet must remain calm and pleasant when dealing with staff and managers. Because they are supervisors, art directors are often called upon to resolve problems, not only with projects but with employees as well.

Art directors are not entry-level workers. They usually have years of experience working at lower-level jobs in the field before gaining the knowledge needed to supervise projects. Art directors in the publishing industry have to know how printing presses operate and how content is created and laid out for online publications. They should also be familiar with a variety of production techniques in order to understand the wide range of ways that images can be manipulated to meet the needs of a project.

REQUIREMENTS

High School

A college degree is usually a requirement for art directors; however, in some instances, it is not absolutely necessary. A variety of high school courses will give you both a taste of college-level offerings and an idea of the skills necessary for art directors on the job. These courses include art, drawing, art history, graphic design, mathematics, Web design, illustration, photography, advertising, and desktop publishing.

Other useful courses that you should take in high school include journalism, business, computing, English, and technical drawing.

Postsecondary Training

According to the American Institute of Graphic Arts, nine out of 10 artists have a college degree. Among them, six out of 10 have majored in graphic design, and two out of 10 have majored in fine arts. In addition, almost two out of 10 have a master's degree. Along with general two- and four-year colleges and universities, a number of professional art schools offer two-, three-, or four-year programs with such classes as figure drawing, painting, graphic design, and other art courses, as well as classes in art history, writing, business administration, communications, and foreign languages.

Courses in journalism, advertising, marketing, photography, layout, desktop publishing, and fashion are also important for those interested in becoming art directors. Specialized courses, sometimes offered only at professional art schools, may be particularly helpful for students who want to go into art direction. These include typography, animation, storyboard, Web site design, and portfolio development.

Because of the rapidly increasing use of computers in design work, it is essential to have a thorough understanding of how computer art and layout programs work. At smaller publishers, the art director may be responsible for operating this equipment; at larger publishers, a staff person, under the direction of the art director, may use these programs. In either case, the director must know what can be done with the available equipment.

In addition to course work at the college level, many universities and professional art schools offer graduates or students in their final year a variety of workshop projects, desktop publishing training opportunities, and internships. These programs provide students with opportunities to develop their personal design styles as well as their portfolios.

Other Requirements

The work of an art director requires creativity, imagination, curiosity, and a sense of adventure. Art directors must be able to work with all sorts of specialized equipment and computer software, such as graphic design programs, as well as make presentations on the ideas behind their work.

The ability to work well with different people is a must for art directors. They must always be up-to-date on new techniques, trends, and attitudes. And because deadlines are a constant part of the work, an ability to handle stress and pressure well is key.

Accuracy and attention to detail are important parts of the job. When art is done neatly and correctly, the public usually pays no notice. But when a publication is done poorly or sloppily, people will notice, even if they have had no design training. Other requirements for art directors include time-management skills and an interest in media and people's motivations and lifestyles.

EXPLORING

High school students can get an idea of what an art director does by working on the staff of the school newspaper, magazine, or yearbook. It may also be possible to secure a part-time job assisting the advertising director of the local newspaper or to work at an advertising agency. Developing your own artistic talent is important, and this can be accomplished through self-training (reading books and practicing) or through courses in painting, drawing, or other creative arts. At the very least, you should develop your "creative eye," that is, your ability to develop ideas visually. One way to do this is by familiarizing yourself with great works, such as paintings or highly creative newspaper and magazine layouts, Web sites, advertisements, motion pictures, videos, or commercials.

Students can also become members of a variety of art or advertising clubs around the nation. Check out the Web site of Paleta: The Art Project (http://www.paletaworld.org) to join a free art club. In addition to keeping members up-to-date on industry trends, such clubs offer job information, resources, and a variety of other benefits.

EMPLOYERS

Approximately 84,200 art directors are employed in the United States. About 18 percent of all art directors are employed at newspaper, magazine, and book publishers throughout the United States. While publishers of all sizes employ art directors, smaller publishers often combine the positions of graphic designer, illustrator, photo editor, and art director. And although opportunities for art direction can be found all across the nation and abroad, many larger publishing companies in such cities as Chicago, New York, and Los Angeles usually have more openings and higher pay scales than smaller publishing companies.

In addition to opportunities in journalism, art directors are employed by advertising agencies, book and magazine publishers, museums, packaging firms, photography studios, marketing and public relations firms, desktop publishing outfits, digital prepress houses, printing companies, film production houses, multimedia developers, computer game developers, and television stations.

STARTING OUT

Since an art director's job requires a great deal of experience, it is usually not considered an entry-level position. Typically, a person on a career track toward art director is hired as an assistant to an established director. Recent graduates wishing to enter the field should have a portfolio of their work containing seven to 10 samples to demonstrate their understanding of the type of publication (newspapers, magazines, or books) and the media (print or online) in which they want to work.

Serving as an intern is a good way to get experience and develop skills. Graduates should also consider taking an entry-level job in an art department at a newspaper or magazine to gain initial experience. Either way, aspiring art directors must be willing to acquire their credentials by working on various projects. This may mean working in a variety of areas, such as advertising, marketing, editing, and design.

College publications offer students a chance to gain experience and develop portfolios. In addition, many students are able to do freelance work while still in school, allowing them to make important industry contacts and gain on-the-job experience at the same time.

ADVANCEMENT

Many people who get to the position of art director do not advance beyond the title but move on to work at more prestigious newspapers and magazines. Competition for positions at well-known newspapers and magazines continues to be keen because of the sheer number of talented people interested. At smaller publications, the competition may be less intense, since candidates are competing primarily against others in the local market.

EARNINGS

According to the U.S. Department of Labor (DOL), beginning art directors or art directors who worked at a small newspaper or magazine earned $41,670 or less per year in 2009. Experienced art directors working at larger newspapers or magazines earned $160,060 or more. Mean annual earnings for art directors employed by newspaper, magazine, book, and directory publishers were $79,720 in 2009. The median annual earnings for art directors working in all industries were $78,580. Again, it is important to note that these positions are not entry level; beginning art directors have probably already accumulated several years of experience in the field for which they were paid far less.

Most publishing companies employing art directors offer insurance benefits, a retirement plan, and other incentives and bonuses.

WORK ENVIRONMENT

Art directors usually work in studios or office buildings. While their work areas are ordinarily comfortable, well lit, and ventilated, they often handle glue, paint, ink, and other materials that may pose safety hazards, and they should, therefore, exercise caution.

Art directors at publishing companies usually work a standard 40-hour week. Many, however, work overtime during busy periods in order to meet deadlines.

While art directors work independently when reviewing artwork and reading copy, much of their time is spent collaborating with and supervising a team of employees, often consisting of editors, photographers, illustrators, graphic artists, and desktop publishing specialists.

OUTLOOK

The extent to which art director positions are in demand, like many other positions, depends on the economy in general; when times are tough, people and media companies spend less, and cutbacks are made. When the economy is healthy, employment prospects for art directors will be favorable. The DOL predicts that employment for art directors will grow about as fast as the average for all occupations through 2018, but declining opportunities in publishing will limit job growth. Publishers always want some type of illustration to enhance their newspapers, magazines, books, and Web sites. People who can quickly and creatively generate new concepts and ideas will be in high demand.

However, it is important to note that competition for art director positions is very strong. And although the Internet is expected to provide some opportunities for artists and art directors, some publishing companies are hiring employees without formal art or design training to operate computer-aided design systems and oversee work.

FOR MORE INFORMATION

For more information on design professionals, contact
American Institute of Graphic Arts
164 Fifth Avenue
New York, NY 10010-5901
Tel: 212-807-1990
http://www.aiga.org

The Art Directors Club is an international, nonprofit organization of directors in advertising, graphic design, interactive media, broadcast design, typography, packaging, environmental design, photography, illustration, and related disciplines. For information, contact

Art Directors Club
106 West 29th Street
New York, NY 10001-5301
Tel: 212-643-1440
http://www.adcglobal.org

For information on the graphic arts, contact

Graphic Artists Guild
32 Broadway, Suite 1114
New York, NY 10004-1612
Tel: 212-791-3400
E-mail: admin@gag.org
http://www.gag.org

For industry statistics, information on diversity, and to view a PowerPoint presentation entitled "Tips on Finding a Job in Magazines," visit the MPA Web site.

MPA—The Association of Magazine Media
810 Seventh Avenue, 24th Floor
New York, NY 10019-5873
Tel: 212-872-3700
E-mail: mpa@magazine.org
http://www.magazine.org

Visit this NASAD Web site for information on schools.

National Association of Schools of Art and Design (NASAD)
11250 Roger Bacon Drive, Suite 21
Reston, VA 20190-5248
Tel: 703-437-0700
E-mail: info@arts-accredit.org
http://nasad.arts-accredit.org

For information on careers in newspapers and industry facts and figures, contact

Newspaper Association of America
4401 Wilson Boulevard, Suite 900
Arlington, VA 22203-1867
Tel: 571-366-1000
http://www.naa.org

For information on design issues in newspapers and other news publications, contact
Society for News Design
424 East Central Boulevard, Suite 406
Orlando, FL 32801-1923
Tel: 407-420-7748
http://www.snd.org

Cartoonists

OVERVIEW

Cartoonists are illustrators who draw pictures and cartoons to amuse, educate, and persuade people. They work for newspapers, magazines, cartoon syndicates, book publishers, and advertising agencies.

HISTORY

Broadly speaking, cartoons and other types of illustration have been used to educate and entertain people since the dawn of time. But it wasn't until the invention of movable metal type by Johannes Gutenberg in about 1450 that cartoons and other illustrations began to reach large audiences. The Protestant Reformer Martin Luther created illustrated pamphlets to convey his ideas about reforming the Roman Catholic Church and distributed them to peasants, most of whom were illiterate. As people realized the power of images in educating the public and influencing their opinions, cartoons and other illustrations began to appear in printed publications throughout Europe.

In the United States, Benjamin Franklin's "Join, or Die" is considered the first political cartoon. Its depiction of a snake severed into eight segments was created to encourage the colonies to cooperate in dealing with the Iroquois Nation at the Albany Congress of 1754. By the Civil War, political cartoons had become increasingly important as a means of conveying opinions and information to the American public. Thomas Nast's pro-Union cartoons were so effective that President Abraham Lincoln called him the North's "best recruiting sergeant." Nast is best known, though, for his satirical cartoons in

QUICK FACTS

School Subjects
Art
Computer science
Journalism

Personal Skills
Artistic
Communication/ideas

Work Environment
Primarily indoors
Primarily one location

Minimum Education Level
High school diploma

Salary Range
$31,853 to $57,400 to $65,345+

Certification or Licensing
None available

Outlook
More slowly than the average

DOT
141

GOE
01.04.01

NOC
5241

O*NET-SOC
27-1013.03

Harper's Weekly from 1869 to 1872 that spotlighted the abuses of power by William "Marcy" Tweed and his Tammany Hall political machine in New York City. When Tweed tried to elude justice by fleeing to Spain, it is said that authorities used Nast's cartoons to help identify Tweed.

In 1894, the continuity strip, which featured a comedic or dramatic story that continued from issue to issue, was invented as a means to boost newspaper circulation. By the late 1890s, newspaper magnates Joseph Pulitzer and William Randolph Hearst were using color comics as supplements in their Sunday papers to increase readership. In 1904, *A. Piker Clerk*, by Clare Briggs, became the first daily comic strip, and was soon followed by many other dailies. In 1912, Hearst created the first syndication agency, which sold reprint rights for articles and comic strips to other newspapers in the United States and abroad. Today, this groundbreaking agency is known as the King Features Syndicate.

As cartoons grew in popularity, cartoonists realized that they needed organizations to represent their professional interests. In 1946, the National Cartoonists Society was founded. Today, it boasts a membership of many of the world's top cartoonists who specialize in creating editorial cartoons, humorous magazine and book illustrations, sports cartoons, comic strips, comic books, comic panels, animation, gag cartoons, greeting cards, and advertising. The Association of American Editorial Cartoonists was founded in

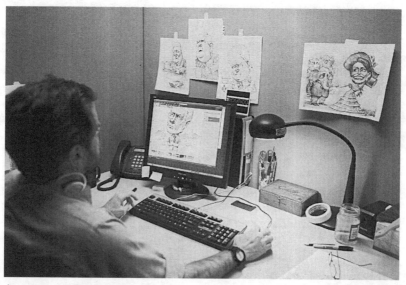

A cartoonist for Politico, a political news Web site, works on a drawing. *(Jacquelyn Martin, AP Photo)*

1957 to promote interest in editorial cartooning and represent the professional interests of editorial cartoonists.

THE JOB

Cartoonists draw illustrations for newspapers, magazines, books, Web sites, greeting cards, and other publications. Cartoons most often are associated with newspaper comics or with editorial commentary, but they are also used to highlight and interpret information in publications as well as in advertising.

Whatever their individual specialty, cartoonists translate ideas onto paper or computer screen in order to communicate these ideas to an audience. Sometimes the ideas are original; at other times they are directly related to the news of the day or to the content of a magazine article. After cartoonists come up with ideas, they discuss them with their employers, who include editors, art directors, or news directors. Next, cartoonists sketch drawings and submit these for approval. Employers may suggest changes, which the cartoonists then make. Cartoonists and illustrators use a variety of art materials, including pens, pencils, markers, crayons, paints, transparent washes, and shading sheets. They may draw on paper, acetate, or bristol board. Some use computers to create their work.

Editorial cartoonists comment on society by drawing pictures with messages that are funny or thoughtful. They often use satire to illuminate the failings or foibles of public figures. Their drawings often depict political or social issues, as well as events in the worlds of sports and entertainment. *Portraitists* are cartoonists who specialize in drawing caricatures. Caricatures are pictures that exaggerate someone's prominent features, such as a large nose, to make them recognizable to the public. Most editorial cartoonists are also talented portraitists.

Comic strip artists tell jokes or short stories in newspapers and magazines with a series of pictures. Each picture is called a frame or a panel, and each frame usually includes words as well as drawings. *Comic book artists* also tell stories with their drawings, but their stories are longer, and they are not necessarily meant to be funny.

Some cartoonists create artwork for full-length illustrated books (called graphic novels). These artists are called *graphic novel artists*.

REQUIREMENTS

High School

If you are interested in becoming a cartoonist, you should study art in high school in addition to following a well-rounded course of study. To comment insightfully on contemporary life, it is useful to study political science, history, and social studies. English and communications classes will also help you to become a better communicator.

Postsecondary Training

Cartoonists need not have a college degree, but employers usually expect some art training. Typical college majors for those who attend college include art, communications, English, or liberal arts. Training in computers in addition to art can be especially valuable. If you are interested in becoming an editorial cartoonist, you should take courses in journalism, history, and political science.

The Center for Cartoon Studies offers a two-year degree that "centers on the creation and dissemination of comics, graphic novels, and other manifestations of the visual narrative." Visit its Web site, http://www.cartoonstudies.org, for more information.

Other Requirements

Cartoonists must be creative. In addition to having artistic talent, they must generate ideas, although it is not unusual for cartoonists to collaborate with writers for ideas. They must be able to come up with concepts and images to which the public will respond. They must have a good sense of humor and an observant eye to detect people's distinguishing characteristics and society's interesting attributes or incongruities.

EXPLORING

View as many cartoons as you can by reading your local paper, visiting the Web sites of newspapers and magazines that feature cartoons, and by reading books that feature the work of top cartoonists.

If you are interested in becoming a cartoonist, draw as much as you can. You should submit your drawings to your school paper or even start your own Web site that showcases your work. You also might want to draw posters to publicize activities, such as sporting events, dances, and meetings.

Student membership in professional associations is another good way to learn more about this career. The Association of American Editorial Cartoonists offers student membership to college students who create editorial cartoons on a regular basis for a college newspaper.

Ask your art teacher to help arrange an information interview with a cartoonist.

EMPLOYERS

Employers of cartoonists include newspapers, magazines, book publishers, cartoon syndicates, and advertising agencies. In addition, a number of these artists are self-employed, working on a freelance basis.

STARTING OUT

Formal entry-level positions for cartoonists are rare, but there are several ways for artists to enter the cartooning field. Most cartoonists begin by working piecemeal, selling cartoons to small publications, such as community newspapers, that buy freelance cartoons. Others assemble a portfolio of their best work and apply to publishers or the art departments of advertising agencies. In order to become established, cartoonists should be willing to work for what equals less than minimum wage. Both the Association of American Editorial Cartoonists and the National Cartoonists Society provide information on breaking into the field at their Web sites.

ADVANCEMENT

Cartoonists' success, like that of other artists, depends on how much the public likes their work. Very successful cartoonists work for prestigious newspapers and magazines at the best wages; some become well known to the public.

EARNINGS

Freelance cartoonists may earn anywhere from $100 to $1,200 or more per drawing, but top dollar generally goes only for big, full-color projects such as magazine cover illustrations. Salaries depend on the work performed. Salary.com reports that earnings for cartoonists ranged from less than $31,853 to $65,345 or more in 2010. Syndicated cartoonists can earn much more. Although the U.S. Department of Labor (DOL) does not give specific information regarding earnings for cartoonists, it does note that the mean earnings for salaried fine artists who worked for newspaper, periodical, directory, and book publishers were $57,400 in 2009. Salaried cartoonists, who are related workers, may have earnings similar to this figure.

Self-employed cartoonists do not receive fringe benefits such as paid vacations, sick leave, health insurance, or pension benefits. Those who are salaried employees of companies, agencies, newspapers, magazines, and the like do typically receive these fringe benefits.

WORK ENVIRONMENT

Most cartoonists work in big cities where employers such as magazine and newspaper publishers are located. They generally work in comfortable environments, at drafting tables, computer workstations, or drawing boards with good light. Staff cartoonists work a regular 40-hour workweek but may occasionally be expected to work evenings and weekends to meet deadlines. Freelance cartoonists have erratic schedules, and the number of hours they work may depend on how much money they want to earn or how much work they can find. They often work evenings and weekends but are not required to be at work during regular office hours.

Cartoonists can be frustrated by employers who curtail their creativity, asking them to follow instructions that are contrary to what they would most like to do. Many freelance cartoonists spend a lot of time working alone at home, but cartoonists have more opportunities to interact with other people than do most working artists.

OUTLOOK

Employment for artists and related workers is expected to grow about as fast as the average for all careers through 2018, according to the DOL. Because so many creative and talented people are drawn to this field, however, competition for jobs will be very strong. Employment for editorial cartoonists who work for newspapers and magazines is expected to be much weaker as a result of industry downsizing and other factors.

About 60 percent of all visual artists are self-employed, but freelance work can be hard to come by, and many freelancers earn little until they acquire experience and establish a good reputation. Competition for work will be keen; those with an undergraduate or advanced degree in art will be in demand. Experience in action drawing and computers are a must.

FOR MORE INFORMATION

Visit the association's Web site to view cartoons and profiles of editorial cartoonists and learn about membership for college students.
Association of American Editorial Cartoonists
3899 North Front Street
Harrisburg, PA 17110-1583
Tel: 717-703-3086
http://editorialcartoonists.com

Visit the society's Web site to read How to Be a Cartoonist, *which features detailed information on how to break into the industry.*

National Cartoonists Society
341 North Maitland Avenue, Suite 130
Maitland, FL 32751-4761
Tel: 407-647-8839
E-mail: info@reuben.org
http://www.reuben.org

This national institution promotes and stimulates interest in the art of illustration by offering exhibits, lectures, educational programs, and social exchange. Contact the society for information on membership for college students, career information, and a list of post-secondary art schools that offer courses, continuing education, or majors in the applied arts of illustration, cartooning, graphic design, or visual communications.

Society of Illustrators
128 East 63rd Street
New York, NY 10065-7303
Tel: 212-838-2560
E-mail: info@societyillustrators.org
http://www.societyillustrators.org

To view a variety of editorial cartoons, visit
Daryl Cagle's Political Cartoonists Index
http://www.cagle.com

Columnists and Commentators

OVERVIEW

Columnists write opinion pieces for publication in newspapers or magazines. Some columnists work for syndicates, which are organizations that sell articles to many media at once. Columnists can be generalists who write about whatever strikes them on any topic. Most columnists focus on a specialty, such as government, politics, local issues, health, humor, sports, gossip, or other themes. Most newspapers employ local columnists or run columns from syndicates. Some syndicated columnists work out of their homes or private offices.

Commentators analyze news and social issues on radio, television, and Internet broadcasts.

HISTORY

Because the earliest American newspapers were political vehicles, much of their news stories brimmed with commentary and opinion. This practice continued up until the Civil War. Horace Greeley, a popular editor who had regularly espoused partisanship in his *New York Tribune,* was the first to give editorial opinion its own page separate from the news.

As newspapers grew into instruments of mass communication, their editors sought balance and fairness on the editorial pages and began publishing a number of columns with varying viewpoints.

Did You Know?

Journalism Web sites are becoming increasingly popular with the public. A study by Nielsen Online for the Newspaper Association of America found that newspaper Web sites "attracted an average monthly unique audience of 72 million visitors in the fourth quarter of 2009, more than one-third (37 percent) of all Internet users." Only a handful of newspapers charge visitors for usage. Look for more newspapers and magazines to begin charging usage fees as companies seek to offset declines in advertising revenue.

Famous Washington, D.C.-based columnist Jack Anderson was known for bringing an investigative slant to the editorial page. Art Buchwald and Molly Ivins were well known for their satirical look at government and politicians. George Will and Fareed Zakaria are known for their keen analysis and opinions about government and world events.

The growth of news and commentary on the Internet has only added to the power of columnists and commentators as their thoughts, ideas, and opinions are read or listened to by millions or even billions throughout the world.

THE JOB

Columnists often take news stories and enhance the facts with personal opinions and panache. Columnists may also write from their personal experiences. Either way, a column usually has a punchy start, a pithy middle, and a strong, sometimes poignant, ending.

Columnists are responsible for writing columns on a regular basis on accord with a schedule, depending on the frequency of publication. They may write a column daily, weekly, quarterly, or monthly. Like other journalists, they face pressure to meet a deadline.

Most columnists are free to select their own story ideas. The need to constantly come up with new and interesting ideas may be one of the hardest parts of the job, but also one of the most rewarding. Columnists search through newspapers, magazines, and the Internet, watch television, and listen to the radio. The various types of media suggest ideas and keep the writer aware of current events and social issues.

David Brooks (*left*), a columnist for the *New York Times*, and Eugene Robinson, a columnist for the *Washington Post*, appear on *Meet the Press*, a weekly news show. *(William B. Plowman/NBC NewsWire via AP Images)*

Next, they do research, delving into a topic much like an investigative reporter would, so that they can back up their arguments with facts.

Finally, they write, usually on a computer. After a column is written, at least one editor goes over it to check for clarity and correct mistakes. Then the cycle begins again. Often a columnist will write a few relatively timeless pieces to keep for use as backups in a pinch, in case a new idea cannot be found or falls through.

Most columnists work in newsrooms or magazine offices, although some, especially those who are syndicated but not affiliated with a particular newspaper, work out of their homes or private offices. Many well-known syndicated columnists work out of Washington, D.C.

Newspapers often run small pictures of columnists, called head shots, next to their columns. This, and a consistent placement of a column in a particular spot in the paper, usually gives a columnist greater recognition than a reporter or editor.

Commentators interpret specific events and discuss how these may affect individuals or the nation. They may have a specified daily slot for which material must be written, recorded, or presented live. They gather information that is analyzed and interpreted through research and interviews and cover public functions such as political conventions, press conferences, and social events. They also may offer commentary on social or cultural issues. In these instances, their commentary is based more on opinion than on fact.

REQUIREMENTS

High School

You will need a broad-based education to be a successful columnist or commentator, so take a college preparatory curriculum in high school. Concentrate on English and journalism classes that will help you develop research, writing, and speaking skills. Keep your computer skills up-to-date with computer science courses. History, psychology, science, and math should round out your education. If you are interested in a specific topic such as sports, politics, or developments in medicine, you should take classes that will help you develop your knowledge in that area. In the future, you will be able to draw on this knowledge when you write your column or present commentary.

Postsecondary Training

As is the case for other journalists, at least a bachelor's degree in journalism is usually required, although some journalists graduate with degrees in political science or English. Experience may be gained by writing for the college or university newspaper and through a summer internship at a newspaper or other publication. It also may be helpful to submit freelance opinion columns to local or national publications. The more published articles, called "clips," you can show to prospective employers, the better.

Other Requirements

Being a columnist or commentator requires similar characteristics to those required for being a reporter: curiosity, a genuine interest in people, the ability to write and/or speak clearly and succinctly, and the strength to thrive under deadline pressure. But as a columnist or commentator, you will also require a certain wit and wisdom, the compunction to express strong opinions, and the ability to take apart an issue and debate it.

You must have a pleasing voice and personality in order to find success as a commentator. Good diction and English usage, thorough knowledge of correct pronunciation, and freedom from regional dialects are very important. A factual error, grammatical error, or mispronounced word can bring letters or e-mails of criticism to station managers. If you plan to work in television broadcasting, you should have a neat appearance and have a combination of sincerity and showmanship that attracts and captures an audience.

EXPLORING

A good way to explore this career is to work for your school newspaper and perhaps write your own column. Participation in debate clubs will help you form opinions and express them clearly. Read your city's newspaper regularly and take a look at national papers as well as magazines. Watch and listen to commentators. Which columnists or commentators, on the local and national level, interest you? Why do you feel their columns or commentaries are well done? Try to incorporate these good qualities into your own writing. Contact your local newspaper or radio or television station and ask for a tour of the facilities. This will give you a sense of what the office atmosphere is like and what technologies are used there. Ask to speak with one of the regular columnists or commentators about his or her job. He or she may be able to provide you with valuable insights. Visit the Dow Jones News Fund Web site (https://www.newsfund.org) for information on careers, summer programs, internships, and more. Try getting a part-time or summer job at the newspaper or radio or television station, even if it is just answering phones and doing data entry. In this way you will be able to test out how well you like working in such an atmosphere.

EMPLOYERS

Newspapers of all kinds run columns, as do certain magazines and even public radio stations, where a recording is played over the airways of the author reading the column. Commentators work for local and national radio and television stations. Some columnists are self-employed, preferring to market their work to syndicates instead of working for a single newspaper or magazine.

STARTING OUT

Most columnists and commentators start out as reporters. Experienced reporters are the ones most likely to become columnists. Occasionally, however, a relatively new reporter may suggest a weekly column or commentary if the beat being covered (for example, politics) warrants it.

Another route for columnists is to start out by freelancing, sending columns out to a multitude of newspapers and magazines in the hopes that someone will pick them up. Also, columns can be marketed to syndicates. A list of these, and magazines that may also be interested in columns, is provided in the *Writer's Market* (http://www.writersmarket.com).

ADVANCEMENT

Newspaper columnists can advance in national exposure by having their work syndicated. They also may try to get a collection of their columns published in book form. Moving from a small newspaper or magazine to a large national publication is another way to advance.

Columnists also may choose to work in other editorial positions, such as editor, editorial writer or page editor, or foreign correspondent.

Most successful commentators advance from small stations to large ones. Experienced commentators usually have held several jobs. The most successful commentators may be those who work for the networks. Usually, because of network locations, commentators must live in or near the country's largest cities. Commentators may also choose to become reporters or news anchors. Some enter the administrative side of the business and become station managers.

EARNINGS

Like reporters' salaries, the incomes of columnists vary greatly according to experience, newspaper size and location, and whether the columnist is under a union contract. But generally, columnists earn higher salaries than reporters.

The U.S. Department of Labor (DOL) classifies columnists with reporters and correspondents, and reports that the median annual income for these professionals was $34,360 in 2009. Ten percent of those in this group earned less than $19,650, and 10 percent made more than $74,700 annually. Popular columnists at large papers earn considerably higher salaries.

The DOL classifies commentators with broadcast news analysts. In 2009, it reports that those employed in radio and television broadcasting earned mean annual salaries of $68,480. Salaries for all broadcast news analysts ranged from less than $24,790 to $138,690 or more.

Freelancers may get paid by the column. Syndicates pay columnists 40 percent to 60 percent of the sales income generated by their columns or a flat fee if only one column is being sold.

Freelancers must provide their own benefits. Columnists working on staff at newspapers and magazines receive typical benefits such as health insurance, paid vacation days, sick days, and retirement plans.

WORK ENVIRONMENT

Columnists and commentators work mostly indoors in newspaper, magazine, or radio and television station offices, although they may occasionally conduct interviews or do research on location out of the office. Some columnists and commentators may work as much as 48 to 52 hours a week.

Some columnists do the majority of their writing at home or in a private office and come to the newsroom primarily for meetings and to have their work approved or changed by editors.

The atmosphere in a newsroom is generally fast paced and loud, so columnists and commentators must be able to concentrate and meet deadlines in this type of environment.

OUTLOOK

The DOL predicts that employment for news analysts, reporters, and correspondents (including columnists) will decline through 2018. Growth will be hindered by such factors as mergers and closures of newspapers, decreasing circulation, and lower profits from advertising revenue. Online publications are a source for new jobs. It is difficult to break into the newspaper and magazine industries, and competition for the position of columnist is even stiffer because these are prestigious jobs that are limited in number. Smaller daily and weekly newspapers may be easier places to find employment than major metropolitan newspapers, and movement up the ladder to columnist will also likely be quicker. Pay, however, is less than at bigger papers. Journalism and mass communication graduates will have the best opportunities, and writers will be needed to replace those who leave the field for other work or retire.

The DOL predicts that employment for broadcast news analysts (a category that includes commentators) will grow more slowly than the average for all careers through 2018. There will be strong competition for jobs at top television and radio stations. Opportunities will be better at smaller stations and on the Internet, but these are often only part-time positions.

FOR MORE INFORMATION

For a list of accredited programs in journalism and mass communications, visit the ACEJMC Web site.
  Accrediting Council on Education in Journalism and Mass
    Communications (ACEJMC)
  University of Kansas School of Journalism and Mass
  Communications
  Stauffer-Flint Hall, 1435 Jayhawk Boulevard
  Lawrence, KS 66045-7575
  Tel: 785-864-3973
  http://www2.ku.edu/~acejmc/STUDENT/PROGLIST.SHTML

Contact the alliance for information on careers in radio and television, as well as scholarships and internships for college students.
  Alliance for Women in Media (formerly American Women in
    Radio and Television)
  1760 Old Meadow Road, Suite 500
  McLean, VA 22102-4306
  Tel: 703-506-3290
  http://www.awrt.org

For information on union membership, contact
  American Federation of Radio and Television Artists
  260 Madison Avenue
  New York NY 10016-2401
  Tel: 212-532-0800
  http://www.aftra.org

For information on careers in nonfiction writing, education, and financial aid opportunities, contact
  American Society of Journalists and Authors
  1501 Broadway, Suite 302
  New York, NY 10036-5505
  Tel: 212-997-0947
  http://www.asja.org

This association provides general educational information on all areas of journalism, including newspapers, magazines, television, and radio.
  Association for Education in Journalism and Mass Communication
  234 Outlet Pointe Boulevard
  Columbia, SC 29210-5667

Tel: 803-798-0271
E-mail: aejmchq@aol.com
http://www.aejmc.com

*An association of university broadcasting faculty, industry profes-
sionals, and graduate students, BEA offers annual scholarships in
broadcasting for college juniors, seniors, and graduate students.
Visit its Web site for useful information about broadcast education
and the broadcasting industry.*
Broadcast Education Association (BEA)
1771 N Street, NW
Washington, DC 20036-2891
Tel: 202-429-3935
http://www.beaweb.org

Contact the association for information on union membership.
National Association of Broadcast Employees and Technicians
501 Third Street, NW
Washington, DC 20001-2760
http://nabetcwa.org

*For information on jobs, scholarships, internships, college pro-
grams, and other resources, contact*
National Association of Broadcasters
1771 N Street, NW
Washington, DC 20036-2800
Tel: 202-429-5300
E-mail: nab@nab.org
http://www.nab.org

*The SPJ has chapters for college students all over the United States
and offers information on scholarships and internships.*
Society of Professional Journalists (SPJ)
3909 North Meridian Street
Indianapolis, IN 46208-4011
Tel: 317-927-8000
http://www.spj.org

*Visit the following Web site for comprehensive information on jour-
nalism careers, summer programs, and college journalism programs:*
High School Journalism
http://www.hsj.org

Copy Editors

OVERVIEW

Copy editors, sometimes called *line editors*, read manuscripts for correct grammatical usage and spelling. They edit the manuscripts to conform with the publisher's style, which includes such points as capitalization, abbreviations, and the use of numbers. They polish the writing style, make sure the style and structure is consistent throughout the manuscript, and flag the text with questions about details that may need elaboration or clarification from the writer. Copy editors are employed by magazine and book publishers, newspapers, newsletters, corporations of all kinds, advertising agencies, radio stations, television stations, and Internet sites. There are approximately 129,600 editors (including copy editors) employed in the United States.

HISTORY

The history of book editing is tied closely to the history of the book and bookmaking and the history of the printing process. The 15th-century invention of the printing press by German goldsmith Johannes Gutenberg and the introduction of movable type in the West revolutionized the craft of bookmaking. Books could now be mass-produced. It also became more feasible to make changes to copy before a book was put into production. Printing had been invented hundreds of years earlier in Asia, but books did not proliferate there as quickly as they did in the West, which saw millions of copies in print by 1500.

In the early days of publishing, authors worked directly with the printer, and the printer was often the publisher and seller of the author's work. Eventually, however, booksellers began to work directly with the authors and took over the role of publisher. The publisher then became the middleman between author and printer.

The publisher worked closely with the author and sometimes acted as the editor. The word *editor*, in fact, derives from the Latin word *edere* or *editum* and means "supervising or directing the preparation of text." Eventually, specialists were hired to perform the editing function. These editors, who were also called advisers or literary advisers in the 19th century, became an integral part of the publishing business.

The editor, also called the sponsor in some houses, sought out the best authors, worked with them, and became their advocate in the publishing house. Some editors became so important that their very presence in a publishing house could determine the quality of author that might be published there. Some author-editor collaborations have become legendary. The field has grown through the 20th and 21st centuries, with computers greatly speeding up the process by which copy editors and other editorial professionals move copy to the printer or to publication online.

In 1997, the American Copy Editors Society was formed to represent the professional interests of copy editors. It has approximately 800 members.

THE JOB

Copy editors read manuscripts carefully to make sure that they are sufficiently well written, factually correct (sometimes this job is done by a researcher or fact checker), grammatically correct, and appropriate in tone and style for its intended readers. If a manuscript is not well written, it is not likely to be well received by readers. If it is not factually correct, it will not be taken seriously by those who spot its errors. If it is not grammatically correct, it will not be understood. If it is not appropriate for its audience, it will be utterly useless. Any errors or problems in a printed piece reflect badly not only on the author but also on the publishing house.

Copy editors use proofreaders' marks to indicate they have found a problem with the manuscript. These marks are universally understood throughout the publishing industry and help editorial professionals quickly communicate potential problems contained in a manuscript.

The copy editor must be an expert in the English language, have a keen eye for detail, and know how to identify problems. The editor will simply correct some kinds of errors, but in some cases—

especially when the piece deals with specialized material—the editor may need to ask, or query, the author about certain points. An editor must never change something that he or she does not understand, since one of the worst errors an editor can make is to change something that is correct to something that is incorrect.

After a copy editor finishes editing a manuscript, it is usually reviewed by a senior copy editor and may be (but is not always) returned to the author for review. Once all parties agree that the manuscript is in its final form, it is prepared for production.

Copy editors in newspaper or magazine publishing may also be required to write headlines for articles and stories. They may make suggestions on how a story or its corresponding illustrations should appear on the page. Copy editors in book publishing are usually required to edit entire manuscripts, including the table of contents, foreword, main text, glossary, bibliography, and index. They may also proofread galleys, proofs, and advertising and marketing materials for errors.

REQUIREMENTS

High School

Copy editors must be expert communicators, so you should excel in English. You must learn to write extremely well, since you will be correcting and even rewriting the work of others. If elective classes in writing are available in your school, take them. Study journalism and take communications courses. Work as a writer or editor for the school paper. Take a photography class. Since virtually all editors use computers, take computer courses. You absolutely must learn to type. If you cannot type accurately and rapidly, you will be at an extreme disadvantage. Do not forget, however, that a successful copy editor must have a wide range of knowledge. The more you know about many areas, the more likely you will be to do well as an editor. Do not hesitate to explore areas that you find interesting. Do everything you can to satisfy your intellectual curiosity. As far as most editors are concerned, there is no useless information.

Postsecondary Training

A copy editor must have a bachelor's degree, and advanced degrees are highly recommended for editors who are interested in moving up in the industry. Most copy editors have degrees in English or journalism, but it is not unheard of for editors to major in one of the other liberal arts. If you know that you want to specialize in a field such as scientific editing, you may wish to major in the area of science of your choice while minoring in English, writing, or journalism. There are many opportunities for editors in technical fields, since most of those who go into editing are interested primarily in the liberal arts. Many colleges offer courses in book editing, magazine design, general editing, and writing. Some colleges, such as the University of Chicago, University of Denver, and Stanford University, offer programs in publishing, and many magazines and newspapers offer internships to students. Take advantage of these opportunities. It is extremely important that you gain some practical experience while you are in school. Work on the school paper or find a part-time job with a newspaper or magazine. Do not hesitate to work for a publication in a noneditorial position. The more you know about the publishing business, the better off you will be.

Other Requirements

Good copy editors are fanatics for the written word. Their passion for good writing comes close to the point of obsession. They are analytical people who know how to think clearly and communicate what they are thinking. They read widely. They not only recognize good English when they see it but also know what makes it good. If they read something they do not understand, they analyze it until they do understand it. If they see a word they do not know, they look it up. When they are curious about something, they take action and research the subject. They are not satisfied with not knowing things.

You must be detail oriented to succeed as a copy editor. You must also be patient, since you may have to spend hours combing manuscripts for inconsistencies and style issues. If you are the kind of person who cannot sit still, you probably will not succeed as a copy editor. To be a good copy editor, you must be a self-starter who is not afraid to make decisions. You must be good not only at identifying problems but also at solving them, so you must be creative. If you are both creative and a perfectionist when it comes to language, copyediting may be the line of work for you.

EXPLORING

One of the best ways to explore the field of editing is to work on a school newspaper or other publication. The experience you gain will definitely be helpful, even if your duties are not strictly editorial. Being involved in writing, reporting, typesetting, proofreading, printing, preparing copy for the Web, or any other task will help you to understand editing and how it relates to the entire field of publishing.

If you cannot work for the school paper, try to land a part-time job with a local newspaper or newsletter. If that does not work, you might want to publish your own newsletter. There is nothing like trying to put together a small publication to help you understand how publishing works. You may try combining another interest with your interest in editing. For example, if you are interested in environmental issues, you might want to start a newsletter that deals with environmental problems and solutions in your community.

Another useful project is keeping a journal. In fact, any writing project will be helpful, since editing and writing are inextricably linked. Write something every day. Try to rework your writing until it is as good as you can make it. Try different kinds of writing, such as letters to the editor, short stories, poetry, essays, comedic prose, and plays.

The American Copy Editors Society offers a wide variety of resources for aspiring and professional copy editors at its Web site (http://www.copydesk.org). These include articles about copyediting, a discussion board, a practice copyediting test, and suggested books and Web sites. The society also offers student membership to high school students who are taking journalism courses or working on a school or alternative publication.

EMPLOYERS

Approximately 129,600 editors (including copy editors) are employed in the United States. One of the best things about the field of editing is that there are many kinds of opportunities for copy editors. The most obvious employers for copy editors are newspaper, magazine, and book publishers. There are many varieties of all three of these types of publishers. There are small and large publishers, general and specialized publishers, local and national publishers. If you have a strong interest in a particular field, you will undoubtedly find various publishers that specialize in it.

Another excellent source of employment is business. Almost all businesses of any size need writers and copy editors on a full-time or part-time basis. Corporations often publish newsletters for their employees or produce publications that talk about how they do business. Large companies produce annual reports that must be written and copyedited. In addition, advertising is a major source of work for copy editors, proofreaders, and writers. Advertising agencies use copy editors, proofreaders, and quality-control people, as do typesetting and printing companies (in many cases, proofreaders edit as well as proofread). Keep in mind that somebody has to work on all the printed and electronic material you see every day, from books and magazines, to menus and matchbooks, to Web sites and text on Smartphones.

STARTING OUT

There is tremendous competition for editorial jobs, so it is important for a beginner who wishes to break into the business to be as well prepared as possible. College students who have gained experience as interns, have worked for publications during the summers, or have attended special programs in publishing will be at an advantage. In addition, applicants for any editorial position must be extremely careful when preparing cover letters and resumes. Even a single error in spelling or usage will disqualify an applicant. Applicants for editorial or proofreading positions must also expect to take and pass tests that are designed to determine their language skills.

Many copy editors enter the field as *editorial assistants* or *proofreaders*. Some editorial assistants perform only clerical tasks, whereas others may also proofread or perform basic editorial tasks. Typically, an editorial assistant who performs well will be given the opportunity to take on more and more editorial duties as time passes. Proofreaders have the advantage of being able to look at the work of editors, so they can learn while they do their own work.

The American Copy Editors Society offers job listings at its Web site, http://www.copydesk.org. Other good sources of information about job openings are school career services offices, classified ads in newspapers and trade journals, specialized publications such as *Publishers Weekly* (http://www.publishersweekly.com), and Internet sites (such as JournalismJobs.com, http://www.journalismjobs.com; NewsLink, http://newslink.org; and Newspapers.com, http://www.newspapers.com).

One way to proceed is to identify local publishers through the Yellow Pages. Many publishers have Web sites that list job openings, and large publishers often have telephone job lines that serve the same purpose.

ADVANCEMENT

After gaining skill and experience, copy editors may be given a wider range of duties while retaining the same title. The may advance to the position of *senior copy editor*, which involves overseeing the work of junior copy editors, or *project editor*. The project editor performs a wide variety of tasks, including copyediting, coordinating the work of in-house and freelance copy editors, and managing the schedule of a particular project. From this position, an editor may move up to become an assistant editor, then managing editor, then editor in chief.

At newspapers, a common advancement route is for copy editors to be promoted to a particular department, where they may move up the ranks to management positions. An editor who has achieved success in a department may become a *city editor*, who is responsible for news, or a *managing editor*, who runs the entire editorial operation of a newspaper.

Magazine copy editors advance in much the same way that copy editors in book publishing do. They work their way up to become senior editors, managing editors, copy chiefs, and editors in chief. In many cases, magazine copy editors advance by moving from a position on one magazine to the same position with a larger or more prestigious magazine. Such moves often bring significant increases in both pay and status.

EARNINGS

Median annual earnings for all editors were $50,800 in 2009, according to the U.S. Department of Labor. The lowest paid 10 percent earned less than $28,430 and the highest paid 10 percent earned $97,360 or more. In 2009, the mean annual earnings for all editors in newspaper, periodical, and book publishing were $58,580, while those employed in radio and television broadcasting earned $56,200.

Copy editors typically receive fringe benefits such as paid vacations, sick leave, health insurance, and pension benefits. Copy editors who work on a freelance basis do not receive these benefits.

WORK ENVIRONMENT

For the most part, publishers of all kinds realize that a quiet atmosphere is conducive to work that requires tremendous concentration. It takes an unusual ability to focus to copyedit in a noisy place. Most copy editors work in private offices or cubicles.

Deadlines are an important issue for copy editors. Newspaper and magazine copy editors often have the most pressing deadlines since these publications may be produced daily or weekly. Copy editors who are employed by publications that have a presence on the Web, especially newspapers, may have to meet countless deadlines during a single day to ensure that readers have the most up-to-date information. Copy editors who are employed by book publishers have more relaxed deadlines since book publishing occurs over the course of months, not days or weeks.

OUTLOOK

According to the *Occupational Outlook Handbook*, employment of all editors will experience little change through 2018. Competition for those jobs will remain intense, since so many people want to enter the field. Book publishing will remain particularly competitive, since many people still view the field in a romantic light. Much of the expansion in publishing is expected to occur in small newspapers and in broadcast media. In these organizations, pay is low even by the standards of the publishing business.

There will be increasing job opportunities for copy editors in Internet publishing as online publishing and services continue to grow. Advertising and public relations will also provide employment opportunities. A fairly large number of positions—both full time and freelance—become available when experienced copy editors leave the business for other fields.

FOR MORE INFORMATION

The following organization's Web site is an excellent source of information about careers in copyediting. ACES organizes educational seminars and maintains lists of internships.

American Copy Editors Society (ACES)
Seven Avenida Vista Grande, Suite B7, #467
Santa Fe, NM 87508-9207
Tel: 415-704-4884
E-mail: info@copydesk.org
http://www.copydesk.org

Visit the society's Web site for information on careers, job fairs, internships, high school journalism resources, diversity programs and to read A Career in Newspapers *and* Why Choose Journalism?: A Guide to Determining if a Career in Newspapers Is Right for You.

American Society of News Editors
11690B Sunrise Valley Drive
Reston, VA 20191-1409
Tel: 703-453-1122
http://www.asne.org

Founded in 1958 by the Wall Street Journal *to improve the quality of journalism education, this organization offers internships, scholarships, and literature for college students. To read* The Journalist's Road to Success: A Career Guide, *which lists schools offering degrees in news-editing and financial aid to those interested in print journalism, visit the DJNF Web site.*

Dow Jones News Fund (DJNF)
PO Box 300
Princeton, NJ 08543-0300
Tel: 609-452-2820
E-mail: djnf@dowjones.com
https://www.newsfund.org

The EFA is an organization for freelance editors, writers, and other publishing professionals. Members receive a newsletter and a free listing in its directory.

Editorial Freelancers Association (EFA)
71 West 23rd Street, 4th Floor
New York, NY 10010-4102
Tel: 212-929-5400
E-mail: office@the-efa.org
http://www.the-efa.org

For comprehensive information for citizens, students, and news people about the field of journalism, visit

Project for Excellence in Journalism
1615 L Street, NW, Suite 700
Washington, DC 20036-5621
Tel: 202-419-3650
E-mail: mail@journalism.org
http://www.journalism.org

Editorial and Research Assistants

QUICK FACTS

School Subjects
English
Journalism

Personal Interests
Communication/ideas
Following instructions

Work Environment
Primarily indoors
Primarily one location

Minimum Education Level
Some postsecondary training

Salary Range
$20,000 to $32,000 to
$50,000

Certification or Licensing
None available

Outlook
Little or no change

DOT
132

GOE
01.02.01

NOC
1452, 4122

O*NET-SOC
27-3041.00

OVERVIEW

Editorial and research assistants perform a wide range of functions, but their primary responsibility is to assist editors with ensuring that text provided by writers is accurate and suitable in content, format, and style for the intended audiences. Editorial and research assistants work for magazines, newspapers, book publishers, newsletters, corporations of all kinds, advertising agencies, radio stations, television stations, and Internet sites.

HISTORY

For as long as newspapers, magazines, and books have been published, editorial and research assistants have helped editors and other publishing professionals to fact check, proofread, and otherwise ensure that articles and other text are appropriate for publication. Although these positions are entry level in nature, they offer an excellent introduction to the world of publishing. Many top journalists and editors broke into the business as editorial and research assistants.

Today's editorial and research assistants use computers and the Internet to help them do their jobs more quickly and effectively. They remain key support workers in publishing, journalism, broadcasting, and other industries.

THE JOB

Editorial and research assistants work for many kinds of publishers, publications, and corporations. They assist editors with the tasks

Books to Read

Hilliard, Robert L., and Michael C. Keith. *The Broadcast Century and Beyond: A Biography of American Broadcasting.* 5th ed. St. Louis, Mo.: Focal Press, 2010.

Kennedy, George, and Daryl Moen. *What Good Is Journalism?: How Reporters and Editors Are Saving America's Way of Life.* Columbia, Mo.: University of Missouri Press, 2007.

Kern, Jonathan. *Sound Reporting: The NPR Guide to Audio Journalism and Production.* Chicago: University of Chicago Press, 2008.

Kovach, Bill, and Tom Rosenstiel. *The Elements of Journalism: What Newspeople Should Know and the Public Should Expect.* Rev. ed. New York: Three Rivers Press, 2007.

Schlachter, Gail Ann, and David R. Weber. *How to Pay for Your Degree in Journalism and Related Fields, 2010–2012.* El Dorado Hills, Calif.: Reference Service Press, 2010.

Starkey, Guy, and Andrew Crisell. *Radio Journalism.* Thousand Oaks, Calif.: Sage Publications Ltd., 2009.

Streisel, Jim. *High School Journalism: A Practical Guide.* Jefferson, N.C.: McFarland & Company Inc., Publishers, 2007.

necessary to provide clearly written, accurate reading material. Both positions tend to be entry-level jobs that may provide the opportunity for advancement. Editorial and research assistants may be assigned to support one editor or writer, an editorial team, or an entire department. They may work on one project at a time or several projects simultaneously.

Editorial assistants perform many different tasks. They may handle the clerical aspects of an editorial project, such as going through the editorial department mail, filing documents, making photocopies, corresponding with authors, and submitting expense reports and invoices to accounting for payment. They may be responsible for obtaining permission to reuse previously published materials such as artwork, maps, tables, or writing from another person, or verifying that the author has already obtained permission. They may also perform other tasks more directly involved with editing, such as reviewing text for style and format issues, correcting any spelling or grammar errors, and adding or deleting content to make the text more readable or to adhere to space specifications. They may be responsible for using desktop publishing software to edit text, photos, or art, and create page layouts.

In addition to the tasks mentioned above, some editorial assistants who work with artists, photographers, and videographers are responsible for writing captions for photographs or videos or labels for artwork. Editorial assistants who work for newspapers may perform basic and formulaic tasks such as updating the winning lottery numbers, sports scores, or calendar events listed in the newspaper, or they may undertake simple writing assignments such as creating birth, engagement, wedding, or anniversary announcements, or obituaries. Editorial assistants who work for book publishers may be responsible for reading through unsolicited manuscripts from writers and determining, which editor, if any, it should be forwarded to for further consideration.

Research assistants generally perform research tasks such as verifying the dates, facts, names of persons and places, and statistics used by a writer. They may review a writer's sources and then verify that the information provided by these sources is correct. They may contact persons interviewed by the writer to ensure that any quotes used by the writer are truthful and correct. Research assistants also contact experts in subject areas pertaining to the topic of the article, often to obtain additional information for the writer, or verify information already used in the article. If a research assistant finds any errors or discrepancies with the writer's text, they are expected to flag and correct them. A research assistant may meet with the writer and/or editor to discuss any discrepancies that are not easily resolved.

Research assistants use a variety of tools to do their jobs. They rely on telephones, fax machines, and computers to obtain the information they need. Researchers may utilize libraries, the Internet, and in-house collections of information as sources of facts, figures, and statistics. Although they may work in a variety of settings, many research assistants work in the magazine/periodical publishing industry.

REQUIREMENTS

High School

Editorial and research assistants must be expert communicators, so you should excel in English. You must learn to write extremely well, since you will be correcting and even rewriting the work of others. If elective classes in writing are available in your school, take them. Take journalism and communications courses. Work as a writer or editor for the school paper. Since virtually all editorial and research assistants use computers, take computer courses and learn how to type quickly and accurately.

Postsecondary Training

Most employers require an editorial assistant to have at least two years of college, and a bachelor's degree is preferred, especially if you wish to advance to a higher position. Research assistants should also have a bachelor's degree. Most editorial workers have degrees in English or journalism, but it is not unheard of to major in one of the other liberal arts. If you know that you want to specialize in a specific field—for example, scientific editing—you may wish to major in an area of science while minoring in English, writing, or journalism. Many colleges offer courses in book editing, magazine design, general editing, and writing. Some colleges, such as the University of Chicago, University of Denver, and Stanford University, offer programs in publishing.

While in college, work on the school paper, literary magazine, or yearbook staff. Many magazines and newspapers offer internships to students interested in editorial work. Find a part-time job with a newspaper or magazine, even if it is a noneditorial position. Take advantage of these opportunities. Everything you can learn about the publishing business will help you find a job later.

Other Requirements

Good editorial and research assistants are fanatics for the written word. They read a lot, across many topics, and know how to think clearly and communicate what they are thinking. When they are curious about something, they take action and research the subject. They are not satisfied with not knowing things.

You must be detail oriented to succeed as an editorial or research assistant. You must also be patient, since you may have to spend hours to painstakingly track down hard-to-find facts and figures. You must be good not only at identifying problems but also at solving them, so you must be creative.

EXPLORING

One of the best ways to explore the editorial and research field is to work for a school newspaper or other publication. Being involved in researching, writing, reporting, proofreading, page layout, printing, or any other task will help you to understand editing and research and how they relate to the entire field of publishing. If you cannot work for the school paper, try to land a part-time job with a local newspaper or newsletter.

Another way to explore the field is by writing, since editing and writing are inextricably linked. You can try keeping a journal, or try other kinds of writing, such as letters to the editor, short stories, poetry, essays, comedic prose, and plays. Write something every day. Try to rework your writing until it is as good as you can make it. This will give you a feel for what an editorial worker does.

EMPLOYERS

One of the best things about the fields of editing and research is that there are many kinds of employment opportunities. The most obvious employers for editorial and research assistants are newspapers, magazines, and book publishers. Most publishers are located in New York City, but many other publishers can be found in large cities across the country. Other employers of editorial and research assistants include advertising agencies; colleges and universities; corporations; museums; nonprofit organizations; local, state, and federal governments; and radio and television news stations.

STARTING OUT

The positions of editorial assistant and research assistant are great opportunities to get your foot in the door of the editorial world. There is tremendous competition for editorial jobs, so it is important for a beginner who wishes to break into the business to be as well prepared as possible. College students who have gained experience as interns, have worked for publications during the summers, or have attended special programs in publishing will be at an advantage. Applicants for editorial positions must also expect to take and pass tests that are designed to determine their language skills.

Good sources of information about job openings are school career services offices, classified ads in newspapers and trade journals, specialized publications such as *Publishers Weekly* (http://publishersweekly.com), and Internet sites. One way to proceed is to identify local publishers through the Yellow Pages. Many publishers have Web sites that list job openings.

ADVANCEMENT

Employees who start as editorial assistants and show promise generally become *editors* or *copy editors*. After gaining skill in that position, they may be given a wider range of duties while retaining the same title. The next step may be a position as an *assistant editor* or *associate editor*, and then *senior editor*. Copy editors may advance to a position such as *senior copy editor*, which involves overseeing the work of junior copy editors. Editors and copy editors may also progress to the position of *project editor*. The project editor performs a wide variety of tasks, including copyediting, coordinating the work of in-house and freelance copy editors, and managing the schedule of a particular project. From this position, a typical line of advancement for an editor may be to move up to become *first assistant editor*, then *managing editor*, then *editor in chief*. These positions involve more management and decision making than is usually found in the positions described previously. The editor in chief works with the publisher to ensure that a suitable editorial policy is being followed, while the managing editor is responsible for all aspects of the editorial department. The assistant editor provides support to the managing editor.

Employees who start as research assistants usually have the same advancement options of editorial assistants, or they may choose to advance within the research department, taking on greater responsibilities and earning a higher salary. Some research assistants, as well as editorial assistants, branch out into careers in writing.

In many cases, editorial workers advance by moving from a position in one company to the same position with a larger or more prestigious company. Such moves may bring significant increases in both pay and status.

EARNINGS

Competition for editorial jobs is fierce, and there is no shortage of people who wish to enter the field. For that reason, companies that employ editorial and research assistants generally pay relatively low wages.

Editorial assistants earn salaries that range from $25,000 at smaller companies to $32,000 at large publishing houses. However, beginning salaries of $20,000 or less are still common in many places. Very experienced editorial assistants may earn as much as $50,000 a year. According to Payscale.com, in 2010 editorial assistants earned median annual salaries that ranged from $27,506 to $35,720.

Earnings of research assistants vary widely, depending on the level of education and the experience of the research assistant and employer. Generally, large companies pay research assistants more than smaller companies and nonprofit organizations do. Self-employed research assistants get paid by the hour or by assignment. Depending on the experience of the research assistant, the complexity of the assignment, and the location of the job, pay rates may be anywhere from $7.25 to $25 per hour, although $10 to $12 is the norm.

Benefits for full-time workers include vacation and sick time, health, and sometimes dental, insurance, and pension or 401(k) plans. Self-employed editorial and research assistants must provide their own benefits.

WORK ENVIRONMENT

The environments in which editorial and research assistants work can vary widely. For the most part, publishers of all kinds realize that a quiet atmosphere is conducive to work that requires tremendous concentration. Most editorial and research assistants work in cubicles. Editorial and research assistants in publishing often work in quieter surroundings than do assistants working for a newspaper or in advertising agencies, who sometimes work in rather loud and hectic situations.

Even in relatively quiet surroundings, however, editorial and research assistants often have many distractions. While working on assignment, an assistant may also have to deal with phone calls from authors, meetings with members of the editorial and production staff, and questions from freelancers, among many other details.

Deadlines are an important issue for all editorial workers. Newspaper and magazine editorial and research assistants face daily or weekly deadlines, whereas those who are employed by book publishers usually have deadlines that are months in length. In almost all cases, though, editorial and research assistants must work long hours during certain phases of the editing process to meet deadlines.

OUTLOOK

The U.S. Department of Labor does not provide employment outlook predictions for editorial and research assistants, but it is estimated that their employment outlook will match that of editors, an occupational group that will experience little or no employment growth through 2018. Competition for those jobs will remain intense, since so many people want to enter journalism-related fields. Opportunities will be best for editorial and research assistants with advanced degrees and experience preparing text, photographs, and video for electronic publication.

FOR MORE INFORMATION

The society represents the professional interests of copy editors who work for newspapers, magazines, Web sites, and other employers. Visit its Web site for information on scholarships for college students, job listings, editing guidelines and quizzes, conferences, and membership for high school and college students.

American Copy Editors Society
Seven Avenida Vista Grande, Suite B7, #467
Santa Fe, NM 87508-9207
Tel: 415-704-4884
E-mail: info@copydesk.org
http://www.copydesk.org

This organization of book publishers offers an extensive Web site to learn about the book business.

Association of American Publishers
71 Fifth Avenue, 2nd Floor
New York, NY 10003-3004
Tel: 212-255-0200
http://www.publishers.org

Visit the fund's Web site for information on print and online journalism careers, college and university journalism programs, high school journalism workshops, scholarships, internships, and job listings.

Dow Jones News Fund
PO Box 300
Princeton, NJ 08543-0300
Tel: 609-452-2820
E-mail: djnf@dowjones.com
https://www.newsfund.org

The EFA is an organization for freelance editors, writers, and other publishing professionals. Members receive a newsletter and a free listing in its directory.

Editorial Freelancers Association (EFA)
71 West 23rd Street, 4th Floor
New York, NY 10010-4102
Tel: 212-929-5400
E-mail: office@the-efa.org
http://www.the-efa.org

Contact this organization for comprehensive information on the magazine publishing industry.

MPA—The Association of Magazine Media
810 Seventh Avenue, 24th Floor
New York, NY 10019-5873
Tel: 212-872-3700
E-mail: mpa@magazine.org
http://www.magazine.org

The nonprofit organization represents the $47 billion newspaper industry and more than 2,000 newspapers in the United States and Canada. Visit its Web site for information on trends in the industry and careers (including digital media job descriptions).

Newspaper Association of America
4401 Wilson Boulevard, Suite 900
Arlington, VA 22203-1867
Tel: 571-366-1000
http://www.naa.org

Fashion Writers and Editors

OVERVIEW

Fashion writers express, promote, and interpret fashion ideas and facts in written form. *Fashion editors* perform a wide range of functions, but their primary responsibility is to ensure that text provided by fashion writers is suitable in content, format, and style for the intended audiences.

HISTORY

Starting around the 14th century, fashion trends were promoted via word of mouth and the exchange of fashion dolls. The development of the printing press by Johannes Gutenberg in the middle of the 15th century fostered the growth of printing publications, which eventually lead to publications dedicated to fashion. The first fashion magazine is generally thought to be a German publication that began in the late 16th century.

Fashion writers and editors were originally employed by newspaper, magazine, and book publishers. As technologies changed, fashion writers and editors began to discuss fashion on television and radio shows. Today, fashion writers and editors have a strong presence on the Web, as well.

THE JOB

Fashion writers, also known as *fashion reporters, correspondents,* or *authors,* express their ideas about fashion in words for books, magazines, newspapers, advertisements, radio, television, and the Internet. These writing jobs require a combination of creativity and hard work.

The majority of fashion writers are employed by fashion magazines. These writers report on fashion news, conduct interviews of top designers, or write feature articles on the latest styles for a season. Fashion writers also work for newspapers with fashion sections (often a part of a larger arts-and-entertainment department), Web sites, or other media outlets.

Good fashion writers gather as much information as possible about their subject and then carefully check the accuracy of their sources. This can involve extensive library research, interviews, and long hours of observation and personal experience. Writers usually keep notes from which they prepare an outline or summary. They use this outline to write a first draft and then rewrite sections of their material, always searching for the best way to express their ideas. Generally, their writing will be reviewed, corrected, and revised many times before a final copy is ready for publication.

Fashion editors work with fashion writers on the staffs of newspapers, magazines, publishing houses, radio or television stations, and corporations of all kinds. Their primary responsibility is to make sure that text provided by fashion writers is suitable in content, format, and style for the intended audiences. For example, a fashion editor working for a newspaper would ensure that articles are timely and can be understood and enjoyed by the newspaper's average reader—not just people in the fashion industry.

Editors must make sure that all text to be printed is well written, factually correct (sometimes this job is done by a researcher or fact checker), and grammatically correct. Other editors, including *managing editors, editors in chief,* and *editorial directors,* have managerial responsibilities and work with heads of other departments, such as marketing, sales, and production.

REQUIREMENTS

High School

Fashion writers and editors must learn to write well, so it is important to take English, journalism, and communications courses in high school. To gain a better perspective on fashion and design, take classes in family and consumer science, including sewing and design, if they are available in your school. Since much of the fashion industry is based overseas, taking classes in a foreign language, such as French, will also be beneficial. Since all editors and writers use computers, take computer courses and learn how to type quickly and accurately.

Postsecondary Training

A college education is usually necessary if you want to become a writer or editor. You should also know how to use a computer for word processing and be able to handle the pressure of deadlines. Employers prefer to hire people who have a communications, English, or journalism degree. Fashion writers and editors must be knowledgeable about their subject, so classes—or even degrees—in fashion design and marketing are also strongly recommended.

Other Requirements

Good fashion editors and writers are analytical people who know how to think clearly and communicate what they are thinking. They must have the ability to conceptualize in two and three dimensions and convey this information to their audience. They are benefited by a working knowledge of clothing construction and an eye for fashion trends. Fashion editors and writers must keep abreast of the latest styles and movements in the fashion industry.

EXPLORING

To improve your writing skills, read as much as you can. Read all kinds of writing—not just fashion articles. Fiction, nonfiction, poetry, and essays will introduce you to many different forms of writing. Try to write every day. Write your own reviews or articles about the latest fashions or trends in the industry. You can also work as a reporter, writer, or editor on school newspapers, yearbooks, and literary magazines.

EMPLOYERS

Fashion writers and editors are typically employed by newspaper, magazine, and book publishers; radio and television stations; and online publications. Some fashion writers and editors are also employed by fashion houses and advertising agencies. In the United States, New York City, San Francisco, Miami, and Los Angeles are major fashion centers. Work also may be found in other U.S. cities, although not as many jobs are available in these locations. Many fashion positions are available in foreign countries.

STARTING OUT

Many fashion writers and editors start out in the industry by gaining experience as an editorial assistant. Typically, an editorial assistant who performs well will be given the opportunity to take on more and more editorial or writing duties as time passes.

The competition for editorial jobs is great, especially in the fashion industry, so it is important for a beginner who wishes to break into the business to be as well prepared as possible. College students who have gained experience as interns, have worked for fashion publications during the summers, or have attended special programs in publishing will be at an advantage.

Jobs may be found through your school's career services office, classified ads in newspapers and trade journals, specialized publications such as *Publishers Weekly* (http://www.publishersweekly.com), and Internet sites. Many publishers have Web sites that list job openings, and large publishers often have telephone job lines that serve the same purpose.

ADVANCEMENT

Employees who start as editorial assistants and show promise may be given a wider range of duties while retaining the same title. Eventually they may become editors or staff writers. They may progress from less significant stories and tasks to important fashion news and feature stories. As they accrue experience, they may be promoted to other editorial or writing positions that come with greater responsibility and pay. They may also choose to pursue managerial positions within the field of fashion editing and writing, such as managing editor and editor in chief. These positions involve more management and decision making than is usually found in the positions described previously. The editor in chief works with the publisher to ensure that a suitable editorial policy is being followed, while the managing editor is responsible for all aspects of the editorial department.

As is the case within many editorial and writing positions, a fashion writer or editor may advance by moving from a position on one publication or company to the same position with a larger or more prestigious publication or company. Such moves may involve an increase in both salary and prestige.

EARNINGS

Beginning fashion writers' salaries range from $20,000 to $26,000 per year. More experienced writers may earn between $28,000 and $38,000. Best-selling authors may make well $100,000 or more per year, but they are few in number. According to the U.S. Department of Labor, median annual earnings for all writers in 2009 were $53,900. The lowest paid 10 percent earned less than $28,070 and the highest paid 10 percent earned $105,710 or more. Writers employed in newspaper, periodical, and book publishing earned mean annual salaries of $53,050.

The salaries of fashion editors are roughly comparable to those of other editors. Median annual earnings for all editors were $50,800 in 2009, according to the U.S. Department of Labor (DOL). The lowest paid 10 percent earned less than $28,400 and the highest paid 10 percent earned $97,360 or more. In 2009, the mean annual earnings for all editors in newspaper, periodical, and book publishing were $58,580, while those employed in radio and television broadcasting earned $56,200. Starting salaries of $20,000 or less are still common in many areas.

Benefits for full-time staff fashion writers and editors include vacation and sick time, health, and sometimes dental, insurance, and pension or 401(k) plans. Self-employed fashion writers and editors must provide their own benefits.

WORK ENVIRONMENT

The environments in which fashion writers and editors work can vary widely. Most writers and editors work in offices or cubicles. But they may not spend all of their time there, as their job may require them to attend fashion shows in other cities, visit fashion houses or department stores, attend social functions, or make less glamorous visits to the library for research. Many of these events happen after the typical 9-to-5 workday is over, or on weekends.

Almost all fashion writers and editors must deal with deadlines, which affects their work environment. Some writers and editors, such as those who work for newspapers or magazines, work in a much more pressurized atmosphere than those working on books because they face daily or weekly deadlines. Fashion editors and writers working on books may have a more regular 40-hour workweek and less constant deadline pressure, since book production usually takes place over several months. In almost all cases, though, fashion writers and editors will work long hours during certain phases of the editing process to meet deadlines.

OUTLOOK

Little change in employment is expected for all editors, while employment for all writers is expected to grow faster than the average for all occupations through 2018, according to the DOL. However, because of the narrow scope of fashion writing and editing, competition for jobs will be very intense. Individuals with previous experience and specialized education in fashion and reporting will be the most successful at finding jobs.

FOR MORE INFORMATION

This organization of book publishers offers an extensive Web site for people interested in learning more about the book business.
Association of American Publishers
71 Fifth Avenue, 2nd Floor
New York, NY 10003-3004
Tel: 212-255-0200
http://www.publishers.org

For information on the industry, student membership, or networking opportunities, contact
Fashion Group International Inc.
Eight West 40th Street, 7th Floor
New York, NY 10018-2276
Tel: 212-302-5511
http://www.fgi.org

This organization is a good source of information on internships and the magazine industry.
MPA—the Association of Magazine Media
810 Seventh Avenue, 24th Floor
New York, NY 10019-5873
Tel: 212-872-3700
E-mail: mpa@magazine.org
http://www.magazine.org

For information on educational programs in fashion, contact
National Association of Schools of Art and Design
11250 Roger Bacon Drive, Suite 21
Reston, VA 20190-5248
Tel: 703-437-0700
E-mail: info@arts-accredit.org
http://nasad.arts-accredit.org

*Visit this site for information on careers in fashion writing and edit-
ing and school listings.*
   Fashion-Schools.org
   http://www.fashion-schools.org

*To read about fashions, models, and agencies, check out this Web
site hosted by fashion magazine* Vogue.
   Style.com
   http://www.style.com

For subscription information, contact
   Women's Wear Daily
   http://www.wwd.com

Food Writers and Editors

QUICK FACTS

School Subjects
Computer science
English
Journalism

Personal Skills
Communication/ideas
Helping/teaching

Work Environment
Primarily indoors
One location with some travel

Minimum Education Level
Bachelor's degree

Salary Range
$28,070 to $53,900 to
$105,710+ (writers)
$28,430 to $50,800 to
$97,360+ (editors)

Certification or Licensing
None available

Outlook
About as fast as the average
(writers)
Little or no change (editors)

DOT
131, 132

GOE
01.01.01, 01.01.02

NOC
5121, 5122

O*NET-SOC
27-3041.00, 27-3043.00

OVERVIEW

Food writers write about food and drink. They may report on food- or cooking-related events, interview chefs or other food/cooking personalities, review recipes or restaurants, or simply write about a specific food or product. With their writing, they may persuade the general public to choose certain goods, services, and personalities.

Food editors perform a wide range of functions, but their primary responsibility is to ensure that text provided by food writers is suitable in content, format, and style for the intended audiences.

Food writers and editors work for magazines, trade journals, newspapers, books, Web sites, and radio and television broadcasts. They may also work as freelancers.

HISTORY

The skill of writing has existed for thousands of years; writing about food has probably existed just as long. Recipes have been found recorded on clay tablets from Mesopotamia dating back more than 3,800 years. One of the oldest surviving cookbooks, *De Re Coquinaria*, is a collection of recipes generally attributed to a Roman gourmet by the name of Marcus Apicius, who lived during the 1st century.

After many centuries of writing recipes and cookbooks, people moved on to writing about food, its preparation, and reviewing food-serving establishments. One of the first magazines in the United States dedicated solely to food and wine, *Gourmet*, was published in 1941. *Gourmet* was also the first U.S. magazine to regularly publish restaurant reviews, something that is quite common now.

Today, there are many magazines devoted to food, and most newspapers have sections devoted to food, as well. Take a walk down the food/cookbook aisle at any bookstore and the sheer number of books and the variety of food topics covered may amaze you. Today, food writers and editors are busier than ever.

THE JOB

Food writers and editors deal with the written word, whether the completed work is the printed page, broadcast, or computer screen. The nature of their work is as varied as the materials they produce: magazine, newspaper, Web site, and trade journal articles; books; advertisements; and scripts for radio and television broadcast. The one common factor is the subject: food.

Food writers need to be able to write very descriptively, since the reader will not be able to taste, touch, or smell the product they are writing about. Depending on whether pictures accompany the written word, the reader may not even be able to see it. Food writers use their writing skills to write about many different things. They might write a press release about a new food product to be distributed to food editors at numerous newspapers and magazines. They may write a story about seasonal fruits and vegetables for a local television news broadcast. They may write an article for a women's magazine about new cooking utensils that make meal preparation easier for amateur chefs. They may write a review about a new restaurant that just opened.

Food writers who work for newspapers or magazines generally write about all things related to food and beverages, such as recipes, new food products, meal planning and preparation, grocery shopping, cooking utensils and related products, and establishments that serve food and beverages. Some food writers also cover other subject areas as well, especially if they work for a newspaper or a general interest magazine, as opposed to a magazine dedicated solely to food.

Perhaps the most infamous type of food writer is the *food/restaurant critic*. The critic needs to be objective and fair with any type of product or restaurant review. When dining at a restaurant, he or she also needs to be anonymous, which is not always easy. While dining, food/restaurant critics need to make accurate observations and try to write or record them without arousing the suspicion of the restaurant staff, lest they realize they are being reviewed.

Food editors need to be able to polish the work of a food writer into a finished article or book. They correct grammar, spelling, and style, and check all the facts, especially where recipes are concerned. They make sure that the writing adheres to any pertinent style guidelines, and that the writing is appropriate for the intended audience. When working for a magazine or newspaper, food editors may also be responsible for planning the editorial content of an entire food section, which can range in size from as little as half of a page to a multiple-page spread. Their duties may include assigning stories to staff or freelance writers, as well as assigning photography or artwork assignments as needed, to accompany the articles and recipes.

Food writers and editors who work for publishing houses may work on tour or guidebooks, writing and editing restaurant reviews and stories about regional food specialties. Or they may work with recipes and cookbooks, meticulously checking to ensure all ingredients and measurements are correct, and that no steps have been omitted from the cooking directions.

Food writers and editors can be employed either as in-house staff or as freelancers. Freelancers must provide their own office space and equipment, such as computers and fax machines. Freelance writers also are responsible for keeping tax records, sending out invoices, negotiating contracts, and providing their own health insurance.

REQUIREMENTS

High School
If you are interested in becoming a food writer or an editor, take English, general science, family and consumer science, and computer classes while in high school. If they are offered at your school, take elective classes in writing or editing, such as journalism and business communications. Editors and writers in any areas must be expert communicators, so you should excel in English. You must learn to write well, since you will be correcting and even rewriting the work of others. While in high school, participating with the school's newspaper, yearbook, or any other publication will be of benefit to you.

Postsecondary Training
Most food writing and editing jobs require a college education. Some employers desire communications or journalism training in college.

Others will require culinary course work. Most schools offer courses in journalism and some have more specialized courses in book publishing, publication management, and newspaper and magazine writing.

Some employers require a degree or certificate from culinary school, or culinary work experience, in addition to a background in writing or editing. You may wish to take cooking classes from a local culinary school or community college to enhance your marketability as a food writer or editor.

In addition to formal course work, most employers look for practical writing and editing experience of any kind. Experience with college newspapers, yearbooks, or literary magazines will give you an edge, as well as if you have worked for small community newspapers or radio stations, even in an unpaid position. Many businesses, book publishers, magazines, newspapers, and radio and television stations have summer internship programs that provide valuable training. Interns do many simple tasks, such as running errands and answering phones, but some may be asked to perform research, conduct interviews, or even write or edit some minor pieces.

Other Requirements

In general, food writers and editors should be creative and able to express ideas clearly. Other assets include curiosity, persistence, initiative, resourcefulness, an accurate memory, and the ability to concentrate and produce quality work under pressure.

One last requirement, perhaps the most obvious, is that you should love food and everything to do with food. As a food writer or editor, you will spend much of your time sampling products, trying recipes, and writing or editing countless numbers of stories about food, so if you are not passionate about the subject, you will not be happy with your job.

EXPLORING

As a high school or college student, explore your interest in the fields of writing and editing by working as a reporter or writer on school newspapers, yearbooks, and literary magazines. If you cannot work for the school paper, try to land a part-time job on a local newspaper or newsletter. Explore your passion for food and increase your knowledge by taking cooking classes, attending ethnic festivals and food events, or touring different food-related businesses. Experiment with different types of restaurants and cuisines. After dining at a new restaurant, write about the experience. Review your writing. Is it objective? Descriptive? Informative? Edit and rewrite it until you are satisfied with it.

Small community newspapers, local radio stations, and food-related Web sites often welcome contributions from outside sources, although they may not be able to pay for them. You could even start your own blog that details your dining experiences. Jobs in bookstores, magazine shops, and even newsstands offer a chance to become familiar with the various publications.

Professional organizations dedicated to food writing and editing, such as those listed at the end of this article, often provide information, resources, conferences, and other guidance programs that may be of interest to you.

EMPLOYERS

Food writers and editors work for a variety of employers. Magazines, newspapers, online publications, television and radio stations, book publishers, food/beverage manufacturing companies, and food/beverage trade associations all hire food writers and editors. Many food writers and editors work on a freelance basis, as well. Most employers are found in large cities such as New York, but virtually any geographical area served by a large newspaper will offer opportunities for a food writer or editor.

STARTING OUT

Most food writers and editors start out in entry-level positions. These jobs may be listed with college career services offices, or they may be obtained by applying directly to the employment departments of individual newspapers, magazines, book publishers, or broadcasting companies. Graduates who previously had internships with these companies often have the advantage of knowing someone who can give them a personal recommendation or inform them of potential job openings before they are made public, thus giving them an edge over the competition. Want ads in newspapers and trade journals or on Web sites of professional associations are another source for jobs.

Some food writers and editors may start out writing and editing in a different subject area, and later choose to work with food when they have more seniority and priority in choosing work assignments. Other food writers and editors gain experience by freelancing, one article or review at a time. Even unpaid assignments can benefit the aspiring food writer or editor. They allow you to build up your portfolio of food-related writing and editing samples and provide contact with the people who may be in a position to hire you at a later time.

ADVANCEMENT

Food writers and editors are usually rewarded with higher profile assignments and increase in salary as they gain experience. For example, food writers may advance by moving from writing short filler copy or covering local events, to writing main features or traveling to cover high-profile industry events. In many cases, food writers and editors advance by moving from a position on one publication to the same position with a larger or more prestigious publication. Such moves may bring significant increases in both pay and status.

Sometimes freelance food writers and editors accept full-time positions with a newspaper or magazine. Such positions are usually offered on the merit of their previous freelance work for a publication. Other freelance food writers and editors may prefer to remain freelancers, but are able to command a higher paycheck because of their reputation and experience.

EARNINGS

In 2009, the median salary for writers, including food writers, was $53,900 a year, according to the U.S. Department of Labor (DOL). The lowest paid 10 percent earned less than $28,070, while the highest paid 10 percent earned $105,710 or more. Mean annual earnings for writers employed in newspaper, periodical, book, and directory publishers were $53,050 in 2009. Those who worked in radio and television broadcasting earned $65,330.

The DOL reports that the median annual salary for editors, including food editors, was $50,800 in 2009. The lowest paid 10 percent earned $28,430 or less, while the highest paid 10 percent earned $97,360 or more.

The International Association of Culinary Professionals compiled a list of median salaries for careers in the culinary field, including the following: cookbook author, $5,000 to $10,000 on their first book; cookbook editor, $27,000 to $85,000 annually; magazine food editor, $41,000 to $80,000 annually; newspaper food editor, $39,000 to $61,000 annually; food writer on staff at a publication, $19,000 to $40,000 annually; freelance food writer, $100 to $1,000 per story. In general, salaries are higher in large cities. Salaries are also dependent on the employer, as larger publications tend to pay more, and the writer or editor's level of experience, as those with many years of experience are able to earn a larger salary.

In addition to their salaries, many food writers and editors receive additional compensation. Most food critics, for example, have the meals they eat at a restaurant for the purpose of a review paid for by their employer. Some food writers and editors also receive travel expenses to cover expenditures such as mileage from driving to cover local events, or airfare and hotel accommodations for covering out-of-town industry events.

WORK ENVIRONMENT

Working conditions vary for food writers. Although the workweek usually runs 35 to 40 hours, many writers work during nontraditional hours or work overtime. Writers often work nights and weekends to cover food and beverage industry events, review restaurants, or to meet deadlines.

Many food writers work independently, but they often must cooperate with artists, photographers, editors, or advertising people who may have differing opinions of how the materials should be prepared and presented.

Physical surroundings range from comfortable private offices to noisy, crowded newsrooms filled with other workers typing and talking on the telephone. Food writers may be able to do much research via the library, Internet, or telephone interviews, but often may travel to local sites, other cities, or even out of the country.

The environments in which food editors work vary widely. Most editors work in private offices or cubicles. Book and magazine food editors often work in quieter surroundings than do newspaper food editors, who sometimes work in rather loud and hectic situations.

As with food writers, virtually all food editors must deal with the demands of deadlines. Newspaper and magazine food editors work in a much more pressurized atmosphere than book food editors because they face daily or weekly deadlines, whereas book production usually takes place over several months. In almost all cases, though, food editors must work long hours during certain phases of the editing process.

OUTLOOK

The employment of writers, including food writers, is expected to increase faster than the average for all occupations through 2018, according to the *Occupational Outlook Handbook*. Employment for all editors is expected to experience little or no change. Individuals entering this field should realize that the competition for jobs is intense and employment growth will not be as strong in this specialty. Students just out of college may especially have difficulty finding employment. However, the subject of food and beverages continues to grow in popularity, thus providing more opportunities for those who wish to pursue a career in food writing and editing.

FOR MORE INFORMATION

The following organization is an excellent source of information about careers in copyediting. ACES organizes educational seminars and maintains lists of internships.

American Copy Editors Society (ACES)
Seven Avenida Vista Grande, Suite B7, #467
Santa Fe, NM 87508-9207
Tel: 415-704-4884
E-mail: info@copydesk.org
http://www.copydesk.org

The following organization's Web site provides information on issues facing food writers and editors, such as ethics, spelling guidelines, and criticism guidelines:

Association of Food Journalists
Seven Avenida Vista Grande, Suite B7, #467
Santa Fe, NM 87508-9207
Tel: 505-466-4742
http://www.afjonline.com

Visit the fund's Web site for information on print and online journalism careers, college and university journalism programs, high school journalism workshops, scholarships, internships, and job listings.

Dow Jones News Fund
PO Box 300
Princeton, NJ 08543-0300
Tel: 609-452-2820
E-mail: djnf@dowjones.com
https://www.newsfund.org

The following is an organization for freelance editors, writers, and other publishing professionals. Members receive a newsletter and a free listing in their directory.

Editorial Freelancers Association
71 West 23rd Street, 4th Floor
New York, NY 10010-4102
Tel: 212-929-5400
E-mail: office@the-efa.org
http://www.the-efa.org

This organization provides a wealth of industry information at its Web site.

International Association of Culinary Professionals
1100 Johnson Ferry Road, Suite 300
Atlanta, GA 30342-1733
Tel: 800-928-4227
E-mail: info@iacp.com
http://www.iacp.com

This organization offers membership for college students, and an online newsletter and magazine at its Web site.

International Food, Wine & Travel Writers Association
1142 South Diamond Bar Boulevard, #177
Diamond Bar, CA 91765-2203
Tel: 877-439-8929
E-mail: admin@ifwtwa.org
http://www.ifwtwa.org

Contact this organization for comprehensive information on the magazine publishing industry.

MPA—The Association of Magazine Media
810 Seventh Avenue, 24th Floor
New York, NY 10019-5873
Tel: 212-872-3700
E-mail: mpa@magazine.org
http://www.magazine.org

Visit the conference's Web site for information on membership and scholarships for college students and answers to frequently asked questions about a career as an editorial writer.

National Conference of Editorial Writers
3899 North Front Street
Harrisburg, PA 17110-1583
Tel: 717-703-3015
E-mail: ncew@pa-news.org
http://www.ncew.org

Foreign Correspondents

OVERVIEW

Foreign correspondents report on news from countries outside of where their newspapers, radio or television networks, or wire services are located. They sometimes work for a particular newspaper, but since today's media are more interested in local and national news, they usually rely on reports from newswire services to handle international news coverage rather than dispatching their own reporters to the scene. Only the biggest newspapers and television networks employ foreign correspondents. These reporters are usually stationed in a particular city and cover a wide territory.

HISTORY

James Gordon Bennett Sr., a prominent U.S. journalist and publisher of the *New York Herald*, was responsible for many firsts in the newspaper industry. He was the first publisher to sell papers through newsboys, the first to use illustrations for news stories, the first to publish stock market prices and daily financial articles, and he was the first to employ European correspondents. Bennett's son, James Gordon Bennett Jr., carried on the family business and in 1871 sent Henry M. Stanley to central Africa to find Dr. David Livingstone, a famous British explorer who had disappeared.

In the early days, even magazines employed foreign correspondents. Famous American poet Ezra Pound, for example, reported from London for *Poetry* and *The Little Review*.

QUICK FACTS

School Subjects
English
Foreign language
Journalism

Personal Skills
Communication/ideas
Helping/teaching

Work Environment
Indoors and outdoors
Primarily multiple locations

Minimum Education Level
Bachelor's degree

Salary Range
$19,650 to $75,000 to
$100,000+

Certification or Licensing
None available

Outlook
Decline

DOT
N/A

GOE
01.03.01

NOC
5123

O*NET-SOC
27-3022.00

The inventions of the telegraph, telephone, typewriter, portable typewriter, the portable laptop computer, satellites, and the Internet all have contributed to the growth of foreign correspondence.

THE JOB

The foreign correspondent is stationed in a foreign country where his or her job is to report on the news there. Foreign news can range from the violent (wars, coups, and refugee situations) to the calm (cultural events and financial issues). Although a domestic correspondent is responsible for covering specific areas of the news, like politics, health, sports, consumer affairs, business, or religion, foreign correspondents are responsible for all of these areas in the country where they are stationed. A China-based correspondent, for example, could spend a day covering trade policy between the United States and China, and the next day on ethnic tensions between Uighurs and Han Chinese.

A foreign correspondent often is responsible for more than one country. For example, one correspondent can be responsible for the entire Middle East, or the continent of Africa. Depending on where he or she is stationed, the foreign correspondent might have to act as a one-person band in gathering and preparing stories. Often he or she is without a support staff and is the only reporter in the region. Therefore, any jobs that would typically be handled by a news assistant or shared among colleagues are solely his or her responsibility.

Other foreign correspondents share areas with colleagues—as in three correspondents teaming up to cover the Far East. Many have a primary area of responsibility and cover other outlying areas on an as-needed basis. With this vast geographic coverage and the variety of news they cover, foreign correspondents often find themselves in different situations and locations on a daily basis.

In covering a story, much time is devoted to conducting research, investigating leads, setting up appointments, making travel arrangements, making on-site observations, and interviewing local people or those involved in the situation. The foreign correspondent often must be experienced in taking photographs or shooting video. If the foreign correspondent works for a radio or television station, he or she might also be responsible for recording the story or going "live" from the scene. Or, they must be skilled in editing and preparing audio back in the studio. This type of correspondent is known as a *broadcast foreign correspondent*.

Foreign correspondents are drawn to conflicts of all kinds, especially war. They may choose to go to the front of a battle to get an

A CNN correspondent files a live report from South Africa. *(Themba Hadebe, AP Photo)*

accurate picture of what is happening. Or they may be able to get the story from a safer position. Sometimes they face weapons trained directly on them. Some correspondents have been injured—and even killed—while covering a story.

Living conditions can be rough or primitive, sometimes with no running water. The job can sometimes be isolating.

After correspondents have interviewed sources and noted observations about an event or filmed it, they put their stories together, writing on computers and using modern technology like the Internet, e-mail, satellite telephones, and fax machines to finish the job and transmit the story to their newspaper, broadcast station, or wire service. Many times, correspondents work out of hotel rooms.

REQUIREMENTS

High School

In addition to English and creative writing needed for a career in journalism, you should study languages, social studies, political science, history, and geography. Initial experience may be gained by working on your school newspaper or yearbook, or taking advantage of study-abroad programs.

Postsecondary Training

In college, pursuing a journalism major is helpful but may not be crucial to obtaining a job as a foreign correspondent. Classes, or even a major, in history, political science, or literature could be beneficial. Economics and foreign language classes are also helpful.

There are more than 1,500 colleges in the United States that offer degrees in journalism. Most of the good journalism graduate schools offer real-life reporting situations—for example, sometimes graduate schools operate radio/television stations, Web sites, or newspapers, which are staffed and managed by students. Visit the Web site of the Accrediting Council on Education in Journalism and Mass Communications (http://www2.ku.edu/~acejmc/STUDENT/PROGLIST .SHTML) for a list of accredited postsecondary training programs in journalism and mass communications.

Other Requirements

To be a foreign correspondent, in addition to a definite love of adventure, you need to be curious about how other people live, diplomatic when interviewing people, have the courage to sometimes confront people on uncomfortable topics, the ability to communicate well, and the discipline to sometimes act as your own boss. You also need to be strong enough to hold up under pressure yet flexible enough to adapt to other cultures.

EXPLORING

Does this type of work interest you? To explore this field, you can begin by honing your skills in different journalism media. Join your high school newspaper staff to become a regular columnist or write special feature articles. Check out your high school's TV station, if it has one, and audition to be an anchor. If your school has a radio station, volunteer to be on the staff there. If your school has a student-maintained Web site, get involved with that project. Gain as much experience as you can using different media to learn about the strengths and weaknesses of each and find out where you fit in best. You can also ask your high school journalism teacher or counselor to help you set up an information interview with a local journalist. Most are happy to speak with you when they know you are interested in their careers. It may be possible to get a part-time or summer job working at a local TV or radio station or at the newspaper office. Competition for these jobs, however, is strong because many college students take such positions as interns and do the work for little or no pay.

EMPLOYERS

Foreign correspondents work for newswire services, such as the Associated Press, United Press International, Reuters, and Agence-France Presse; major metropolitan newspapers; news magazines; and television and radio networks. These media are located in the largest cities in the United States and in the case of Reuters and Agence-France Presse, in Europe.

STARTING OUT

College graduates have a couple of paths to choose between to become a foreign correspondent. They can decide to experience what being a foreign correspondent is like immediately by going to another country, perhaps one whose language is familiar to them, and freelancing or working as a stringer. That means writing stories and offering them to anyone who will buy them. This method can be hard to accomplish financially in the short run but can pay off substantially in the long run.

Another path is to take the traditional route of a journalist and try to get hired upon graduation at any newspaper, radio station, or television station you can. It helps in this regard to have worked at a summer internship during your college years. Recent college graduates generally get hired at small newspapers or media stations, although a few major metropolitan dailies will employ top graduates for a year with no guarantee of their being kept on afterward. After building experience at a small paper or station, a reporter can try to find work at progressively bigger ones. Reporters who find employment at a major metropolitan daily that uses foreign correspondents can work their way through the ranks to become one.

ADVANCEMENT

Foreign correspondents can advance to other locations that are more appealing to them or that offer a bigger challenge. Or they can return home to become columnists, editorial writers, editors, or network news directors.

EARNINGS

Salaries vary greatly depending on the publication, network, or station, and the cost of living and tax structure in various places around the world where foreign correspondents work. Generally, salaries range from $50,000 to an average of about $75,000 to a peak of $100,000 or more.

According to the U.S. Department of Labor, correspondents and other news reporters earned a median salary of $34,360 in 2009. The lowest paid 10 percent earned $19,650 or less, and the highest paid 10 percent earned $74,700 or more.

Benefits for salaried foreign correspondents depend on the employer; however, they usually include such items as health insurance and retirement or 401(k) plans. Some media will pay for living expenses, such as the costs of a home, school for the reporter's children, and a car. Self-employed correspondents must provide their own benefits.

WORK ENVIRONMENT

Correspondents and other reporters may face a hectic work environment if they have tight deadlines and have to produce their reports with little time for preparation. Correspondents who work in countries that face great political or social problems risk their health and even their lives to report breaking news. Covering wars, political uprisings, fires, floods, and similar events can be extremely dangerous.

Working hours vary depending on the correspondent's deadlines. Their work often demands irregular or long hours. Because foreign correspondents report from international locations, this job involves travel. The amount of travel depends on the size of the region the correspondent covers.

OUTLOOK

Because of consolidations, mergers, decreasing circulation, and increasing operating expenses, employment at newspapers and magazines is expected to decline through 2018. A similar trend is occurring in broadcast organizations. Opportunities may be slightly better at online news organizations, but the pay is much lower than at traditional news organizations and positions are often part time.

Factors that keep the number of foreign correspondents low are the high cost of maintaining a foreign news bureau and the relative lack of interest Americans show in world news. Despite these factors, the number of correspondents is not expected to decrease much more. There are simply too few as it is; decreasing the number could put the job in danger of disappearing, which most journalists believe is not an option. For now and the near future, most job openings will arise from the need to replace those correspondents who leave the job.

FOR MORE INFORMATION

For a list of accredited programs in journalism and mass communications, visit the ACEJMC Web site.

Accrediting Council on Education in Journalism and Mass
    Communications (ACEJMC)
University of Kansas School of Journalism and Mass
Communications
Stauffer-Flint Hall, 1435 Jayhawk Boulevard
Lawrence, KS 66045-7575
Tel: 785-864-3973
http://www2.ku.edu/~acejmc/STUDENT/PROGLIST.SHTML

The society provides information on careers in reporting, as well as details on education and financial aid (from outside sources).

American Society of Journalists and Authors
1501 Broadway, Suite 302
New York, NY 10036-5505
Tel: 212-997-0947
http://www.asja.org

This organization provides general educational information on all areas of journalism, including newspapers, magazines, television, Internet, and radio. Members include journalism and mass communication faculty, administrators, students, and media professionals.

Association for Education in Journalism and Mass
    Communication
234 Outlet Pointe Boulevard
Columbia, SC 29210-5667
Tel: 803-798-0271
E-mail: aejmchq@aol.com
http://www.aejmc.com

Visit the fund's Web site for information on print and online journalism careers, college and university journalism programs, high school journalism workshops, scholarships, internships, and job listings.

Dow Jones News Fund
PO Box 300
Princeton, NJ 08543-0300
Tel: 609-452-2820
E-mail: djnf@dowjones.com
https://www.newsfund.org

The association provides information on broadcast education, scholarships for college students, jobs, and useful publications at its Web site.

National Association of Broadcasters
1771 N Street, NW
Washington, DC 20036-2800
Tel: 202-429-5300
E-mail: nab@nab.org
http://www.nab.org

The guild is a union for journalists, advertising sales workers, and other media professionals.

The Newspaper Guild-Communications Workers of America
501 Third Street, NW, 6th Floor
Washington, DC 20001-2797
Tel: 202-434-7177
E-mail: guild@cwa-union.org
http://www.newsguild.org

This professional organization has represented the interests of international journalists since 1939. Visit its Web site for information on scholarships and membership for college students and journalism resources.

Overseas Press Club of America
40 West 45th Street
New York, NY 10036-4202
Tel: 212-626-9220
http://www.opcofamerica.org

Visit the society's Web site for information on student chapters and scholarships for college students, job listings, training opportunities, educational resources, discussion boards and blogs, and much more.

Society of Professional Journalists
3909 North Meridian Street
Indianapolis, IN 46208-4011
Tel: 317-927-8000
http://www.spj.org

Visit the following Web site for comprehensive information on journalism careers, summer programs, and college journalism programs:

High School Journalism
http://www.hsj.org

For comprehensive information for citizens, students, and news people about the field of journalism, visit
Project for Excellence in Journalism
1615 L Street, NW, Suite 70
Washington, DC 20036-5621
Tel: 202-419-3650
E-mail: mail@journalism.org
http://www.journalism.org

═══ INTERVIEW ═══

Joel Brinkley is a former reporter, editor, and foreign correspondent for the New York Times *and is currently the Visiting Hearst Professional in Residence at Stanford University. In 1980, he won the Pulitzer Prize for International Reporting. Joel discussed his career and the work of foreign correspondents with the editors of* Careers in Focus: Journalism.

Q. What are the most important personal and professional qualities for foreign correspondents?

A. The principle qualities for foreign correspondence are the same as for any reporter—honesty, tenacity, persistent curiosity, and the resolution to be fair. But foreign correspondents must also be vigilant in their determination not to judge other countries, other governments, by the standards and norms of their own country. You should try to judge a country by the standards of its own people, not by the standards of the American people.

Q. What advice would you give to young people who are interested in becoming foreign correspondents?

A. By whatever means you can—university programs abroad, internships, or freelance writing assignments—try working in another country for a few weeks or months. The Associated Press and Reuters hire locally based reporters in foreign countries. Foreign newspapers, Web sites, and broadcast stations hire foreign interns. See if the experience captures you—or scares you. A warning, though: Many people form a lifelong attachment to the first place they work. So pick your country carefully.

Q. What is the employment outlook for foreign correspondents?

A. The employment outlook looks bleak, and in some respect it is. Very few newspapers still maintain foreign bureaus. Television networks have cut back their foreign presence dramatically. But new Web sites, like GlobalPost, are expanding opportunities. The news industry is in transition; we can't tell now what medium will be dominant in the years to come. But foreign coverage is a critical part of journalism. New means of covering the world will develop and mature.

Q. What has been one of your most interesting experiences as a foreign correspondent?

A. I have served as a foreign correspondent for more than 30 years and have worked in more than 50 nations on five continents. I can't even count the amazing adventures I have experienced. But I suppose the most rewarding experience was my first one, reporting from Cambodia in 1979, just after the fall of the Khmer Rouge regime. There, I found hundreds of thousands of miserable refugees who had poured out of Cambodia just after Vietnam invaded and pushed the Khmer Rouge out of power. They told terrible stories of deprivation and death. This was the world's first look at the horror the Khmer Rouge regime had wrought on its people. I contracted typhoid, but still wrote a compelling series of stories. Above, I said that many young reporters form a lifeline attachment to the country they first cover. Well, 30 years later I returned to Cambodia and decided to write a book about the state.

Journalism Teachers

OVERVIEW

Journalism teachers teach students the rudiments of journalistic writing. They develop teaching outlines and lesson plans, give lectures, facilitate discussions and activities, keep class attendance records, assign homework, and evaluate student progress. They teach at the secondary and postsecondary levels.

HISTORY

The first American newspaper, *Publick Occurrences Both Foreign and Domestick*, appeared in Boston in 1690, but lasted only one issue due to censorship by the British government. The first continuously published paper in America was the *Boston News-Letter*, first published in 1704. The first daily newspaper, the *Pennsylvania Evening Post*, began publication in 1783.

Despite a long tradition of newspaper journalism in the United States, it was not until 1869 that the first journalism course was offered at Washington College (now known as Washington and Lee University). In the following decades, a number of colleges and universities, most located in the Midwest, began offering journalism courses.

In 1903, Joseph Pulitzer, a newspaper magnate, gave Columbia University an endowment of $2 million to start a school of journalism. Despite the generous endowment, Columbia was unable to implement and start its new program until 1912. The first school of journalism in the United States—and the world—was founded in 1908 by Walter Williams,

QUICK FACTS

School Subjects
English
Journalism

Personal Skills
Communication/ideas
Helping/teaching

Work Environment
Primarily indoors
Primarily one location

Minimum Education Level
Bachelor's degree

Salary Range
$33,880 to $52,200 to $104,100+

Certification or Licensing
Voluntary (certification)
Required for certain positions (licensing)

Outlook
About as fast as the average (high school teachers)
Faster than the average (college professors)

DOT
090

GOE
12.03.02, 12.03.03

NOC
4121

O*NET-SOC
25-1122.00, 25-2031.00

at the University of Missouri. Educators at the Missouri School of Journalism taught students using a hands-on approach in which they actually published a newspaper. (The school is still producing high-quality graduates today.)

In the early years of the 20th century, schools of journalism grew in popularity on our nation's campuses, and graduate journalism programs were introduced in the 1930s.

Today, journalism and communications programs (which often offer journalism majors) are extremely popular on our nation's campuses. The field of journalism has come a long way from its beginnings in the newspaper industry. The invention of radio, television, and the Internet have created countless opportunities for aspiring journalists, as well as the journalism teachers who prepare students for these careers.

THE JOB

High School Teachers

High school teachers who teach journalism may teach a variety of English courses, including journalism, or they may only teach journalism classes. Most high school journalism classes focus on the fundamentals of journalistic writing.

In the classroom, journalism teachers rely on a variety of teaching methods. They spend a great deal of time lecturing, but they also facilitate student discussion and develop projects and activities to interest the students in journalism. They make use of newspapers and other periodicals, show films and videos, use computers and the Internet, and bring in guest speakers. They assign writing exercises and other projects. Journalism teachers often require their students to spend some amount of time working on the school's newspaper or yearbook.

Outside of the classroom, journalism teachers prepare lectures, lesson plans, and exams. They evaluate student work and calculate grades. In the process of planning their class, journalism teachers read newspapers and magazines and monitor other new sources, such as television, radio, and the Internet to determine class assignments; photocopy notes, articles, and other handouts; and develop grading policies. They also continue to study alternative and traditional teaching methods to hone their skills. They prepare students for special events and conferences and submit student work to competitions. Journalism teachers also have the opportunity for extracurricular work as advisers to the school's publications, such as the newspaper or yearbook.

A high school journalism teacher helps a student at a computer during journalism class. *(George Nikitin, AP Photo)*

College Professors

Members of college and university faculty educate undergraduate or graduate students, or in some cases, both, in their areas of specialty. Journalism professors teach students about the fundamentals of journalistic writing, as well as more specialized topics such as investigative reporting, editorial writing, features writing, media criticism, and journalistic ethics. Some schools do not have a separate journalism department; many times journalism classes are taught under the auspices of the communications department.

The primary duty of a professor is his or her commitment to the students' education. Instruction takes place in the form of classroom lectures and in hands-on activities such as the actual publication of a newspaper, operation of a student-run television or radio station, or the creation of a news-based Web site. Textbooks usually supplement in-class learning, as do assignments, writing laboratories, exams, computers, local and national newspapers, and closed-circuit or cable television. Most professors teach three or four classes each week, totaling 12 to 16 hours weekly. Much of a professor's time is spent preparing lectures and grading papers and exams, an additional two or three hours per class.

Journalism professors may also act as advisers for students. They set a certain amount of time aside to help students schedule a beneficial program of study, answer questions regarding their major, or any other aspects of college life. Not all professors serve as advisers; those who do may have a reduced teaching schedule to compensate.

Serving on department committees is another part of a professor's job. Topics such as academic or departmental issues, department budgets, equipment, new hires, or course curricula are often raised and discussed. Research and publishing both are very important responsibilities for professors. Publishing is a necessity to get and keep tenure-track positions. Tenure is a teaching status granted after a trial period that protects teachers from being fired without just cause. Professors who conduct research usually publish their findings in academic journals or books. In fact, many textbooks are written by college and university faculty.

REQUIREMENTS

High School

To prepare for a career as a journalism teacher—or, in fact, most any other kind of teacher—take a wide variety of college preparatory classes, including science, history, computer science, English, and journalism. Prepare yourself to be comfortable speaking in front of people by taking speech classes or joining your school's speech or debate team.

Postsecondary Training

If you want to be a journalism teacher, your college training will depend on the level at which you plan to teach. All 50 states and the District of Columbia require public high school teachers to have a bachelor's degree in either education or in the subject they teach. Prospective teachers must also complete an approved training program, which combines subject and educational classes with work experience in the classroom, called student teaching.

For prospective college or university professors, you will need at least one advanced degree in your chosen field of study. The master's degree is considered the minimum standard, and graduate work beyond the master's is usually desirable. If you hope to advance in academic rank above instructor, most institutions require a doctorate. Your graduate school program will be similar to a life of teaching—in addition to attending seminars, you will research, prepare articles for publication, and teach some undergraduate courses.

Certification or Licensing

Journalism teachers and professors might consider becoming certified by the Journalism Education Association (see the end of this article for contact information). Although it is not required, certification may boost an individual's attractiveness to employers during the job search.

High school teachers who work in public schools must be licensed under regulations established by the state in which they are teaching. If moving, teachers have to comply with any other regulations in their new state to be able to teach, though many states have reciprocity agreements that make it easier for teachers to change locations.

Licensure examinations test prospective teachers for competency in basic subjects such as mathematics, reading, writing, teaching, and other subject matter proficiency. In addition, many states are moving toward a performance-based evaluation for licensing. In this case, after passing the teaching examination, prospective teachers are given provisional licenses. Only after proving themselves capable in the classroom are they eligible for a full license.

Another growing trend spurred by recent teacher shortages in some elementary and high schools is alternative licensure arrangements. For those who have a bachelor's degree but lack formal education courses and training in the classroom, states can issue a provisional license. These workers immediately begin teaching under the supervision of a licensed educator for one to two years and take education classes outside of their working hours. Once they have completed the required course work and gained experience in the classroom, they are granted a full license.

College and university professors and high school teachers in private schools do not need to be licensed.

Other Requirements

Journalism teachers must respect their students as individuals, with personalities, strengths, and weaknesses of their own. They must also be patient and self-disciplined to manage a large group independently. Teachers should also be well organized, as you will have to keep track of the work and progress of a number of different students.

If you aim to teach at the college level, you should enjoy reading, writing, and researching. Not only will you spend many years studying in school, but your whole career will be based on communicating your thoughts and ideas. People skills are important because you will be dealing directly with students, administrators, and other faculty members on a daily basis. You should feel comfortable in a role of authority and possess self-confidence.

EXPLORING

To explore a teaching career, look for leadership opportunities that involve working with children. You might find summer work as a counselor in a summer camp, as a leader of a scout troop, or as an assistant in a public park or community center. To get some firsthand teaching experience, volunteer for a tutoring program. To explore the area of journalism, join the newspaper or yearbook staff while in high school.

If you are interested in becoming a college professor, spend some time on a college campus to get a sense of the environment. Write to colleges or visit their Web sites to review their admissions brochures and course catalogs; read about the journalism or communications faculty members and the courses they teach. Before visiting college campuses, make arrangements to speak to journalism professors who teach courses that interest you. These professors may allow you to sit in on their classes and observe.

EMPLOYERS

There are 1.1 million secondary teachers employed in the United States. Journalism teachers make up a small percentage of this number. Although rural areas maintain schools, more teaching positions are available in urban or suburban areas. Journalism teachers are also finding opportunities in charter schools, which are smaller, deregulated schools that receive public funding.

There are approximately 29,900 postsecondary communications teachers (including journalism professors) employed in the United States. The majority of all college professors are employed in public and private four-year colleges and universities and two-year community colleges. Employment opportunities vary based on area of study and education. With a doctorate, a number of publications, and a record of good teaching, journalism professors should find opportunities in universities all across the country.

STARTING OUT

While in college and graduate school, prospective journalism teachers should become familiar with their school's career services office to keep abreast of current teaching positions and journalism-related internships available. They should also consider joining associations such as the Journalism Education Association, Investigative Reporters and Editors, and the Society of Professional Journalists. These organizations offer many resources, as well as provide informative meetings and conferences, which can also serve as great networking opportunities.

Prospective high school teachers can use their college career services offices and state departments of education to find job openings. Many local schools advertise teaching positions in newspapers. Another option is to contact the administration in the schools in which you would like to work directly. While looking for a full-time position, you can work as a substitute teacher.

Prospective college professors should start the process of finding a teaching position while in graduate school. You will need to develop a curriculum vitae (a detailed academic resume), work on your academic writing, assist with research, attend conferences, and gain teaching experience and recommendations. Because of the competition for tenure-track positions, you may have to work for a few years in temporary positions. Some professional associations maintain lists of teaching opportunities in their areas. They may also make lists of applicants available to college administrators looking to fill an available position. These lists are often available on the associations' Web sites. The College and University Professional Association for Human Resources, for example, maintains a job list at its Web site, http://www.cupahr.org. Another resource is the *Chronicle of Higher Education* (http://chronicle.com), a newspaper with national job listings that is available in print and online.

ADVANCEMENT

As high school journalism teachers acquire experience or additional education, they can expect higher wages and more responsibilities. Teachers with leadership skills and an interest in administrative work may advance to serve as principals or supervisors, though the number of these positions is limited and competition is fierce. In some high school systems, experienced teachers can become senior or mentor teachers. They help newer, less experienced teachers adjust to teaching, while continuing to maintain their own teaching duties. The additional responsibilities of serving as a mentor usually come with a higher rate of pay. Another move may be into higher education, teaching education classes at a college or university. For most of these positions, additional education is required.

At the college level, the normal pattern of advancement is from instructor to assistant professor, to associate professor, to full professor. All four academic ranks are concerned primarily with teaching and research. Some journalism teachers may choose to enter the administrative side of the field. A doctorate is not necessary, though helpful, at two-year colleges. It is an absolute necessity at four-year colleges and universities, as are service on departmental committees, research and publication, and a stellar teaching record. Some positions to consider are college president, dean, and departmental chairperson.

Some journalism teachers choose to leave the field for more lucrative careers in publishing or business. Many maintain a successful writing career running parallel to their teaching career.

EARNINGS

According to the U.S. Department of Labor (DOL), the median annual salary for high school teachers, including journalism teachers, was $52,200 in 2009. The lowest paid 10 percent earned less than $34,600, and the highest paid 10 paid percent earned $82,000 or more.

High school journalism teachers can often earn additional pay by working with students in extracurricular activities, such as acting as an adviser to the school newspaper or yearbook; coaching sports; or teaching summer school. Other activities that can increase a teacher's salary include acting as a mentor to inexperienced teachers, or earning a master's degree or national certification.

College professors' earnings vary depending on their academic department, the size of the school, the type of school (public, private, women's only), and by the level of position the professor holds. According to the DOL, the median annual salary for college and university communications teachers, including journalism teachers, was $58,890 in 2009. The lowest 10 paid percent earned less than $33,880, and the highest paid 10 percent earned $104,100 or more.

In its 2008–09 salary survey, the American Association of University Professors reported that the average yearly income for all full-time faculty was $79,439. It also reported that professors earned the following average salaries by rank: full professors, $108,749; associate professors, $76,147; assistant professors, $63,827; instructors, $45,977; and lecturers, $52,436.

College journalism professors often have additional earnings from activities such as research, writing for publication in scholarly journals, working in the field as a journalist, or other employment. In addition, many college and university full-time faculty members may have access to campus facilities, tuition waivers for dependents, housing and travel allowances, and paid sabbatical leaves. Part-time faculty members usually have fewer benefits.

WORK ENVIRONMENT

Most journalism teachers are contracted to work 10 months out of the year, with a two-month vacation during the summer. During their summer break, many continue their education to renew or upgrade their teaching licenses and earn higher salaries. Teachers in schools that operate year-round work eight-week sessions with one-week breaks in between and a five-week vacation in the winter.

High school journalism teachers work in generally pleasant conditions, although some older schools may have poor heating or electrical systems. The work can seem confining, requiring them to remain in the classroom throughout most of the day. Teachers may sometimes need to focus more on discipline issues with their students instead of actually teaching, which can be frustrating.

High school hours are generally 8:00 A.M. to 3:00 P.M., but journalism teachers work more than 40 hours a week teaching, preparing for classes, grading papers, and directing extracurricular activities. Similarly, most college journalism teachers work more than 40 hours each week, but their hours may vary. Many may teach classes in the evening or on the weekends. Although they may teach only two or three classes a semester, they spend many hours preparing for lectures, examining student work, and conducting research.

OUTLOOK

According to the *Occupational Outlook Handbook (OOH)*, employment opportunities for high school teachers, including journalism teachers, are expected to grow about as fast as the average for all occupations through 2018. The need to replace retiring teachers will provide many opportunities nationwide, but the demand will vary widely depending on geographic area. Inner-city schools characterized by poor working conditions and low salaries often suffer a shortage of teachers, as do remote, rural areas.

The *OOH* predicts that employment for college and university professors, including journalism professors, will grow faster than the average for all careers through 2018. College enrollment is projected to grow due to an increased number of 18- to 24-year-olds, an increased number of adults returning to college, and an increased number of foreign-born students, thus requiring the need for more college and university professors. Retirement of current faculty members will also provide job openings. However, it is predicted that many of the positions will be part time, and competition for full-time, tenure-track positions at four-year schools will be very strong.

FOR MORE INFORMATION

For information about careers, education, and union membership, contact the following organizations:

American Association of University Professors
1133 19th Street, NW, Suite 200
Washington, DC 20036-3655
Tel: 202-737-5900
E-mail: aaup@aaup.org
http://www.aaup.org

American Federation of Teachers
555 New Jersey Avenue, NW
Washington, DC 20001-2029
Tel: 202-879-4400
http://www.aft.org

National Council for Accreditation of Teacher Education
2010 Massachusetts Avenue, NW, Suite 500
Washington, DC 20036-1023
Tel: 202-466-7496
http://www.ncate.org

National Education Association
1201 16th Street, NW
Washington, DC 20036-3290
Tel: 202-833-4000
http://www.nea.org

This organization provides general educational information on all areas of journalism, including newspapers, magazines, television, Internet, and radio. Members include journalism and mass communication faculty, administrators, students, and media professionals.

Association for Education in Journalism and
　　Mass Communication
234 Outlet Pointe Boulevard, Suite A
Columbia, SC 29210-5667
Tel: 803-798-0271
E-mail: aejmchq@aol.com
http://www.aejmc.com

Visit this organization's Web site for information on investigative journalism and scholarships and membership for college students.

Investigative Reporters and Editors
Missouri School of Journalism
141 Neff Annex
Columbia, MO 65211-0001
Tel: 573-882-2042
http://www.ire.org

The association represents the interests of journalism teachers and publications advisers (at the high school and college levels), media professionals, adviser organizations, press associations, libraries, yearbook companies, newspapers, radio stations, and departments of journalism. Visit its Web site for information on certification, membership for college students, and a mentorship program for new journalism teachers.

Journalism Education Association
Kansas State University
103 Kedzie Hall
Manhattan, KS 66506-1501
Tel: 866-532-5532
http://www.jea.org

Visit the society's Web site for information on student chapters and scholarships for college students, job listings, training opportunities, educational resources, discussion boards and blogs, and much more.

Society of Professional Journalists
3909 North Meridian Street
Indianapolis, IN 46208-4011
Tel: 317-927-8000
http://www.spj.org

Magazine Editors

QUICK FACTS

School Subjects
English
Journalism

Personal Interests
Communication/ideas
Helping/teaching

Work Environment
Primarily indoors
Primarily one location

Minimum Education Level
Bachelor's degree

Salary Range
$28,430 to $50,800 to
$97,360+

Certification or Licensing
None available

Outlook
Little or no change

DOT
132

GOE
01.02.01

NOC
5122

O*NET-SOC
27-3041.00

OVERVIEW

Magazine editors plan the contents of a magazine, assign articles, and select photographs and artwork to enhance the message of the articles. They also edit, organize, and sometimes rewrite the articles. They are responsible for making sure that each issue is attractive, readable, and maintains the stylistic integrity of the publication. Approximately 61,110 editors are employed by newspaper, periodical, book, and directory publishers in the United States.

HISTORY

For the most part, the magazines that existed before the 19th century were designed for relatively small, highly educated audiences. In the early 19th century, however, inexpensive magazines that catered to a larger audience began to appear. At the same time, magazines began to specialize, targeting specific audiences. That trend continues today.

Beginning in the 19th century, magazine staffs became more specialized. Whereas in early publishing a single person would perform various functions, in 19th century and later publishing, employees performed individual tasks. Instead of having a single editor, for example, a magazine would have an editorial staff. One person would be responsible for acquisitions, another would copyedit, another would be responsible for editorial tasks related to production, and so forth.

The publishing industry has also been powerfully affected by technology. Publishing came into existence only after Johannes Gutenberg had invented the necessary technology, and it has changed in various ways as technology has developed. The most important recent developments have been those that have made it possible to transfer and manipulate information rapidly and efficiently. The development of the computer has revolutionized the running of

Yellow Journalism

The phrase "yellow journalism" refers to the style of journalism that began in the late 19th century, describing melodramatic and sensationalized reporting—sometimes greatly exaggerated or even false—in order to sell newspapers. It has roots in the newspaper rivalry between Joseph Pulitzer's *New York World* and William Randolph Hearst's *New York Journal*.

The name itself was taken from a cartoon character, the "Yellow Kid," that first appeared in Pulitzer's *World* in the first comic strip ever, Richard F. Outcault's "Hogan's Alley." Hearst soon lured Outcault, as well as other *World* staffers, to the *Journal* and had him continue the popular comic strip for his paper. Pulitzer found someone else to draw the strip and soon both papers had a version of the popular "Yellow Kid," driving sales of the rival newspapers and giving birth to the moniker "yellow journalism."

The qualities and characteristics of yellow journalism, however, encompassed much more than a cartoon character in yellow. The phrase came to be associated with a colorful, melodramatic style of reporting—sometimes pushing the boundaries of truthfulness with lurid claims—and over-the-top headlines designed to draw a reader to the publication and choose it over the competition. Both the *New York World* and *New York Journal* used the style to some extent, and many newspapers throughout the United States emulated this approach to the news. Hearst used this sensationalized style of reporting while his paper was covering the Cuban struggle for independence against Spain in the late 1890s, and as a result, the *Journal* was quite successful in stirring up American anger at Spanish activities in Cuba. In fact, some historians assert that the ensuing Spanish-American War in 1898 was driven by the fact that Hearst's paper riled the American public, who were outraged by what they read in the *Journal* and demanded that the United States intervene in the conflict there.

In addition to the style of reporting and writing, physical characteristics of a publication are also associated with the era of yellow journalism, including several that are still used today: colorful comics, supplements, plentiful illustrations, and banner headlines designed to grab attention.

Sources: PBS.org, Britannica.com, YellowJournalism.net

magazines and other publications. The worldwide scope of magazine reporting is, of course, dependent upon technology that makes it possible to transmit stories and photographs almost instantaneously from one part of the world to another.

Finally, the Internet has provided an entirely new medium for magazines. Readers can read many magazines online. Online publishers avoid paper and printing costs, but still collect revenue from online subscriptions and advertising.

THE JOB

The duties of a magazine editor are numerous, varied, and unpredictable. The editor determines each article's placement in the magazine, working closely with the sales, art, and production departments to ensure that the publication's components complement one another and are appealing and readable.

Most magazines focus on a particular topic, such as fashion, news, or sports. Current topics of interest in the magazine's specialty area dictate a magazine's content. In some cases, magazines themselves set trends, generating interest in topics that become popular. Therefore, the editor should know the latest trends in the field that the magazine represents.

Depending on the magazine's size, editors may specialize in a particular area. For example, a fashion magazine may have a beauty editor, features editor, short story editor, and fashion editor. Each editor is responsible for acquiring, proofing, rewriting, and sometimes writing articles.

After determining the magazine's contents, the editor assigns articles to writers and photographers. The editor may have a clear vision of the topic or merely a rough outline. In any case, the editor supervises the article from writing through production, assisted by copy editors, assistant editors, fact checkers, researchers, and editorial assistants. The editor also sets a department budget and negotiates contracts with freelance writers, photographers, and artists.

The magazine editor reviews each article, checking it for clarity, conciseness, and reader appeal. Frequently, the editor edits the manuscript to highlight particular items. Sometimes the magazine editor writes an editorial to stimulate discussion or mold public opinion. The editor also may write articles on topics of personal interest.

Other editorial positions at magazines include the *editor in chief*, who is responsible for the overall editorial course of the magazine; the *executive editor*, who controls day-to-day scheduling and

David Remnick, a Pulitzer Prize-winning journalist and the editor of *The New Yorker* magazine, checks layout proofs in his office. *(Ron Haviv, AP Photo)*

operations; and the *managing editor*, who coordinates copy flow and supervises production of master pages for each issue.

Many magazines now have a presence on the Web; some are only available online. As magazine publishers create online editions, *online editors* have come to play a crucial role at magazines. This type of editor selects and updates online content (text, audio, video) as well as coordinates the graphic look of the pages. They are sometimes called multimedia editors. Online editors may be supervised by online producers. Online editors also work for television and radio stations that have a presence on the Web.

Some entry-level jobs in magazine editorial departments are stepping-stones to more responsible positions. Editorial assistants perform various tasks such as answering phones and correspondence, setting up meetings and photography shoots, checking facts, and typing manuscripts. *Editorial production assistants* assist in coordinating the layout of feature articles edited by editors and art designed by art directors to prepare the magazine for printing.

Many magazines hire *freelance writers* to write articles on an assignment or contract basis. Most freelance writers write for several different publications; some become contributing editors to one or more publications to which they contribute the bulk of their work.

Magazines also employ researchers, sometimes called *fact checkers*, to ensure the factual accuracy of an article's content. Researchers may be on staff or hired on a freelance basis.

REQUIREMENTS

High School

While in high school, develop your writing, reading, and analyzing skills through English and composition classes. It will also benefit you to be current with the latest news and events of the world, so consider taking history or politics classes. Reading the daily newspaper and news magazines can also keep you fresh on current events and will help you to become familiar with different styles of journalistic writing.

If your school offers journalism classes or, better yet, has a school newspaper, get involved. Any participation in the publishing process will be great experience, whether you are writing articles, proofreading copy, or laying out pages.

Postsecondary Training

A college degree is required for entry into this field. A degree in journalism, English, or communications is the most popular and standard degree for a magazine editor. The Accrediting Council on Education in Journalism and Mass Communications offers a list of accredited journalism programs at its Web site, http://www2.ku.edu/~acejmc/STUDENT/PROGLIST.SHTML. Specialized publications prefer a degree in the magazine's specialty, such as chemistry for a chemistry magazine, and experience in writing and editing. A broad liberal arts background is important for work at any magazine.

Most colleges and universities offer specific courses in magazine design, writing, editing, and photography. Related courses might include newspaper and book editing.

Other Requirements

All entry-level positions in magazine publishing require a working knowledge of typing and word processing, plus a superior command of grammar, punctuation, and spelling. Deadlines are important, so commitment, organization, and resourcefulness are crucial.

Editing is intellectually stimulating work that may involve investigative techniques in politics, history, and business. Magazine editors must be talented wordsmiths with impeccable judgment. Their decisions about which opinions, editorials, or essays to feature may influence a large number of people.

Handling stress and deadlines, as well as being able to work with and motivate others, is also important. Good reporting skills and a natural curiosity will help editors have good news judgment and instincts. There is always deadline pressure and always news to edit. Although the long hours and pressure are sometimes difficult to handle, the rewards of being an editor are many. In fact, many editors thrive on this unrelenting pressure and excitement.

Good public relations skills are also important for magazine editors. If readers are upset about what they read, or do not read, it is often the editor who has to address their concerns. Although it is good news for a local magazine when the public feels a strong ownership in the publication, it can also be a challenge to meet the needs of a diverse readership.

EXPLORING

The best way to get a sense of magazine editing is to work on a high school newspaper or newsletter. You will probably start out as a staff writer, but with time and experience, you may be able to move into an editorial position with more responsibility and freedom to choose the topics to cover. Other ways to learn about the field include reading books about editing, taking a tour of a magazine's editorial offices, and asking your journalism teacher to arrange an information interview with a magazine editor.

EMPLOYERS

Approximately 61,110 editors are employed by newspaper, periodical, book, and directory publishers in the United States. Major magazines are concentrated in New York, Chicago, Los Angeles, Boston, Philadelphia, San Francisco, and Washington, D.C., while professional, technical, and union publications are spread throughout the country.

STARTING OUT

Competition for editorial jobs can be fierce, especially in the popular magazine industry. Recent graduates hoping to break into the business should be willing to work in other staff positions before moving into an editorial position.

Many editors enter the field as editorial assistants or proofreaders. Some editorial assistants perform only clerical tasks, whereas others may also proofread or perform basic editorial tasks. Typically, an editorial assistant who performs well will be given the opportunity to take on more and more editorial duties as time passes. Proofreaders have the advantage of being able to look at the work of editors, so they can learn while they do their own work.

Good sources of information about job openings are school career services offices and classified ads in newspapers, specialized publications such as *Publishers Weekly* (http://www.publishersweekly.com), and corporate and career-oriented Web sites.

ADVANCEMENT

Employees who start as editorial assistants or proofreaders and show promise generally become copy editors. Copy editors work their way up to become senior editors, managing editors, and editors in chief. In many cases, magazine editors advance by moving from a position on one magazine to the same position with a larger or more prestigious magazine. Such moves often bring significant increases in both pay and status.

EARNINGS

According to the U.S. Department of Labor, the median annual earnings for salaried editors were $50,800 in 2009. The middle 50 percent earned between $37,340 and $71,090. Salaries ranged from less than $28,430 to more than $97,360. Senior editors at large-circulation magazines average more than $100,000 a year. In addition, many editors supplement their salaried income by doing freelance work.

Full-time editors receive vacation time, medical insurance, and sick time, but freelancers must provide their own benefits.

WORK ENVIRONMENT

Most magazine editors work in quiet offices or cubicles. However, even in relatively quiet surroundings, editors can face many distractions. An editor who is trying to copyedit or review the editing of others may, for example, have to deal with phone calls or e-mails from authors, questions from junior editors, meetings with members of the editorial and production staff, and questions from freelancers, among many other demands.

An often stressful part of the magazine editor's job is meeting deadlines. Magazine editors work in a much more pressurized atmosphere than book editors because they face daily or weekly deadlines, whereas book production usually takes place over several months. Many magazine editors must work long hours during certain phases of the publishing cycle.

OUTLOOK

The recent economic recession has hit the magazine industry hard. Declining advertising revenue has caused many magazines to lay off workers. Additionally, rising printing costs have forced some magazines to reduce the number of issues printed or transition their print products to electronic-only publications.

Despite these developments, magazine publishing remains a dynamic industry. In fact, more than 80 percent of American adults read magazines, according to MPA—The Association of Magazine Media. Magazines are launched nearly every day of the year, although the majority fail. According to MPA, 734 new magazines were introduced in 2009. The future of magazines is secure since they are a critical medium for advertisers. Magazine advertising revenue exceeded $19 billion in 2009, according to the MPA.

A recent trend in magazine publishing is focus on a special interest. There is increasing opportunity for employment at special interest, trade, and association magazines for those whose backgrounds complement a magazine's specialty. Internet publishing will provide increasing job opportunities as more businesses develop online publications. The number of magazines with Web sites grew from 10,131 in 2005 to 15,204 in 2009, according to the MPA. Magazine editing is keenly competitive, however, and as with any career, the applicant with the most education and experience has a better chance of getting the job. The *Occupational Outlook Handbook* projects that employment for all editors will experience little or no change through 2018.

FOR MORE INFORMATION

The society is a membership organization for editors of print and online magazines. Visit its Web site for information on internships for college students and to read the Magazine Handbook.

American Society of Magazine Editors
810 Seventh Avenue, 24th Floor
New York, NY 10019-5873
Tel: 212-872-3700
E-mail: asme@magazine.org
http://www.magazine.org/asme

Visit the society's Web site for information on careers, job fairs, internships, high school journalism resources, and diversity programs.
American Society of News Editors
11690B Sunrise Valley Drive
Reston, VA 20191-1409
Tel: 703-453-1122
http://www.asne.org

Visit this organization's Web site for information on investigative journalism and scholarships and membership for college students.
Investigative Reporters and Editors
Missouri School of Journalism
141 Neff Annex
Columbia, MO 65211-0001
Tel: 573-882-2042
E-mail: info@ire.org
http://www.ire.org

Contact this organization for comprehensive information on the magazine publishing industry.
MPA—The Association of Magazine Media
810 Seventh Avenue, 24th Floor
New York, NY 10019-5873
Tel: 212-872-3700
E-mail: mpa@magazine.org
http://www.magazine.org

Visit the following Web site for comprehensive information on journalism careers, summer programs, and college journalism programs:
High School Journalism
http://www.hsj.org

For comprehensive information for citizens, students, and news people about the field of journalism, visit
Project for Excellence in Journalism
1615 L Street, NW, Suite 700
Washington, DC 20036-5621
Tel: 202-419-3650
E-mail: mail@journalism.
http://www.journalism.org

News Anchors

OVERVIEW

News anchors, also *called news analysts* and *newscasters*, broadcast news for radio and television stations. They help select, write, and present the news and may specialize in a particular area. Interviewing guests, making public service announcements, and conducting panel discussions may also be part of the news anchor's work. Approximately 8,000 people are employed as news anchors at radio and television stations in the United States.

HISTORY

Guglielmo Marconi, a young Italian engineer, first transmitted a radio signal in his home in 1895. Radio developed rapidly as people began to comprehend the tremendous possibilities. The stations KDKA in Pittsburgh and WWWJ in Detroit began broadcasting in 1920. Within 10 years, there were radio stations in all the major cities in the United States, and broadcasting became big business. In 1926 the National Broadcasting Company became the first network when it linked together 25 stations across the country. The Columbia Broadcasting System was organized in the following year. In 1934, the Mutual Broadcasting Company was founded. The years between 1930 and 1950 may be considered the zenith years of the radio industry. With the coming of television, radio broadcasting took second place in importance as entertainment for the home—but radio's commercial and communications value should not be underestimated.

Discoveries that led to the development of television can be traced as far back as 1878, when William Crookes invented a tube

Michele Norris (1961–)

Michele Norris has had rich and varied career in journalism, working in print, radio, and television. In 2002 she became the first African American female host for National Public Radio (NPR), hosting the long-running news program *All Things Considered*.

Norris first attended the University of Wisconsin, where she majored in electrical engineering. She later earned her degree from the University of Minnesota in Minneapolis in 1985, where she studied journalism. After college, Norris reported for several newspapers, including the *Chicago Tribune*, *Los Angeles Times*, and *Washington Post*. A series of stories she did for the *Washington Post* about a six-year-old child who lived in a crack house was later reprinted in the book *Ourselves Among Others* (1988), a collection of writings that included essays by many prominent international figures. In 1993, she became a correspondent for ABC News, a position she would hold until 2002, when she became co-host of NPR's *All Things Considered*, the highly acclaimed radio program of news, features, and commentary. During her career, Norris has focused her reporting on such topics as education, poverty, the country's drug problem, and issues affecting the inner city.

Norris has won many awards for her work, including Emmy and Peabody awards for her coverage of the 9/11 attacks, and the National Association of Black Journalists' Salute to Excellence Award for her coverage of Hurricane Katrina. In 2009, she received the National Association of Black Journalists' Journalist of the Year award.

Source: National Public Radio

that produced the cathode ray. Other inventors who contributed to the development of television were Vladimir Zworykin, a Russian-born scientist who came to this country at the age of 20 and is credited with inventing the iconoscope before he was 30; Charles Jenkins, who invented a scanning disk, using certain vacuum tubes and photoelectric cells; and Philo Farnsworth, who invented an image dissector. WNBT and WCBW, the first commercially licensed television stations, went on the air in 1941 in New York. Both suspended operations during World War II but resumed them in 1946 when television sets began to be manufactured on a commercial scale.

As radio broadcasting was growing across the country in its early days, the need for news anchors grew. They identified the station and brought continuity to broadcast time by linking one program with the next as well as participating in many programs. When television began, many radio announcers and newscasters started to work in the new medium. The emergence of cable television and the Internet has opened up new opportunities for news anchors.

THE JOB

News anchors specialize in presenting the news to the listening or viewing public. They report the facts and may sometimes be asked to provide editorial commentary. They may write their own scripts or rely on the station's writing team to write the script, which they then read over the TelePrompTer. Research is important to each news story and the news anchors should be well informed about each story they cover as well as those they simply introduce. News anchors may also report the news, produce special segments, and conduct on-the-air interviews and panel discussions. At small stations, they may even keep the program log, run the transmitter, and cue the changeover to network broadcasting.

News anchors are faced with constant deadlines, not only for each newscast to begin, but also for each one to end. Each segment must be viewed and each script must be read at the precise time and for a specified duration during the newscast. While they must appear calm, professional, and confident, there is often much stress and tension behind the scenes.

Although they perform similar jobs, radio and television news anchors work in very different atmospheres. On radio, the main announcers or anchorpeople are often the *disc jockeys*. They play recorded music, announce the news, provide informal commentary, and serve as a bridge between the music and the listener. They announce the time, weather, news, and traffic reports while maintaining a cheerful and relaxed attitude. At most stations, the radio announcers also read advertising information or provide the voices for the advertising spots.

For *television news anchors*, research, writing, and presenting the news is only part of the job. Wardrobe, make-up, and presentation are major components of a television anchor's job. Many details such as which hairstyles and which outfits to wear are important to create an effective look for the news.

Some radio or television news anchors specialize in certain aspects of the news such as health, economics, politics, or community affairs. Other anchors specialize in sports. These people cover sports

Contessa Brewer, a news anchor for *MSNBC Live*, reports the news. *(Virginia Sherwood/NBCU Photo Bank via AP Images)*

events and must be highly knowledgeable about the sports they are covering as well as having an ability to describe events quickly and accurately as they unfold. *Sports anchors* generally travel to the events they cover and spend time watching the teams or individuals practice and participate. They research background information, statistics, ratings, and personal interest information to provide the audience with the most thorough and interesting coverage of each sports event.

The Internet and the World Wide Web are changing the job of news anchors in radio and television. Many radio and television stations have their own Web sites where listeners and viewers can keep updated on current stories, e-mail comments and suggestions, and even interact with the anchors and reporters. Also, the World Wide Web has become another resource for anchors as they research their stories.

Because their voices and faces are heard and seen by the public on a daily basis, many radio and television news anchors become well-known public personalities. This means that they are often asked to participate in community activities and other public events.

REQUIREMENTS

High School

In high school, you should focus on a college preparatory curriculum that will teach you how to write and speak and use the English language in literature and communication classes. Subjects such as history, government, economics, and a foreign language are also important. Participation in journalism clubs and on your school newspaper will also help you prepare for this career.

Postsecondary Training

Today, most news anchors have earned at least a bachelor's degree in journalism, English, political science, economics, telecommunications, or communications. Visit the Web site of the Accrediting Council on Education in Journalism and Mass Communications (http://www2.ku.edu/~acejmc/STUDENT/PROGLIST.SHTML) for a list of accredited postsecondary training programs in journalism and mass communications.

Other Requirements

Aspiring radio and television news anchors must have a mastery of the English language—both written and spoken. Their diction, including correct grammar usage, pronunciation, and minimal regional dialect, is extremely important. News anchors need to have a pleasing personality and voice, and, in the case of television anchorpeople, they must also have a pleasing appearance.

News anchors need to be creative, inquisitive, aggressive, and should know how to meet and interact with people—including coworkers and people who they interview to help gather the news.

EXPLORING

If you are interested in a career as a news anchor, try to get a summer job at a radio or television station. Although you will probably not have the opportunity to broadcast, you may be able to judge whether or not the type of work appeals to you as a career.

Any chance to speak or perform before an audience should be welcomed. Join the speech or debate team to build strong speaking skills. Appearing as a speaker or performer can show whether or not you have the stage presence necessary for a career in front of a microphone or camera.

Many colleges and universities have their own radio and television stations and offer courses in radio and television. You can gain valuable experience working at college-owned stations. Some radio stations, cable systems, and TV stations offer financial assistance, internships, and co-op work programs, as well as scholarships and fellowships.

EMPLOYERS

Of the roughly 8,000 news anchors working in the United States, almost all are on staff at one of the 14,355 radio stations or 1,785 television stations around the country. Some, however, work on a freelance basis on individual assignments for networks, stations, advertising agencies, and other producers of commercials.

Some companies own several television or radio stations; some stations belong to networks such as ABC, CBS, NBC, or FOX, while others are independent. While radio and television stations are located throughout the United States, major markets where better-paying jobs are found are generally near large metropolitan areas.

STARTING OUT

Most news anchors start in jobs such as production assistant, researcher, or reporter in small stations. As opportunities arise, it is common for anchors to move from one job to another. Network jobs are few, and the competition for them is great. You must have several years of experience as well as a college education to be considered for these positions.

You must audition before you will be employed as a news anchor. You should carefully select audition material to show a prospective employer the full range of your abilities. In addition to presenting prepared materials, you may be asked to read material that you have not seen previously, such as a commercial, news release, dramatic selection, or poem.

ADVANCEMENT

Radio and television news anchors move up by moving on. In other words, one of the main ways to advance within the industry is to move to a larger market or larger station. The ultimate goal of many news anchors is to advance to the network level. Others advance by becoming news directors, station managers, or producers.

EARNINGS

Median annual earnings of all radio and television announcers (including news anchors) were $27,520 in 2009, according to the U.S. Department of Labor (DOL). Salaries ranged from less than $16,070 to $76,340 or more. Broadcast news analysts earned salaries ranging from $24,790 or less to $138,690 or more, with median salaries of $50,400. Top news anchors in large media markets such as New York or Chicago can earn more than $1 million annually.

For both radio and television, salaries are higher in larger markets. Salaries are also generally higher in commercial broadcasting than in public broadcasting. Nationally known news anchors who appear regularly on network television programs receive salaries that may be quite impressive. For those who become top television personalities in large metropolitan areas, salaries also are quite high.

Benefits for news anchors depend on the employer; however, they usually include such items as health insurance, retirement or 401(k) plans, and paid vacation days.

WORK ENVIRONMENT

Work in radio and television stations is usually very pleasant. Almost all stations are housed in modern facilities. The maintenance of technical electronic equipment requires temperature and dust control, and people who work around such equipment benefit from the precautions taken to preserve it.

News anchors' jobs may provide opportunities to meet well-known people or celebrities. Being at the center of an important communications medium can make the broadcaster more keenly aware of current issues and divergent points of view than the average person.

News anchors may report for work at a very early hour in the morning or work late into the night. Some radio stations operate on a 24-hour basis. All-night news anchors may be alone in the station during their working hours.

OUTLOOK

Competition for entry-level employment in announcing during the coming years is expected to be keen, as the broadcasting industry always attracts more applicants than are needed to fill available openings. There is a better chance of working in radio than in television because there are more radio stations. Local television stations usually carry a high percentage of network programs and need only a very small staff to carry out local operations. There will also be increasing opportunities for news anchors in online and mobile news divisions.

The DOL predicts that opportunities for news anchors will grow more slowly than the average for all careers through 2018 due to the slowing growth of new radio and television stations. Openings will result mainly from those who leave the industry or the labor force. The trend among major networks, and to some extent among many smaller radio and TV stations, is toward specialization. News anchors who specialize in such areas as business, sports, weather, consumer news, and health news should have an advantage over other job applicants.

FOR MORE INFORMATION

For a list of accredited programs in journalism and mass communications, visit the ACEJMC Web site.
   Accrediting Council on Education in Journalism and
      Mass Communications (ACEJMC)
   University of Kansas School of Journalism and Mass
      Communications
   Stauffer-Flint Hall, 1435 Jayhawk Boulevard
   Lawrence, KS 66045-7575
   Tel: 785-864-3973
   http://www2.ku.edu/~acejmc/STUDENT/PROGLIST.SHTML

Contact the alliance for information on careers in radio and television, as well as scholarships and internships for college students.
   Alliance for Women in Media (formerly American Women in
      Radio and Television)
   1760 Old Meadow Road, Suite 500
   McLean, VA 22102-4306
   Tel: 703-506-3290
   http://www.awrt.org

For information on union membership, contact
   American Federation of Radio and Television Artists
   260 Madison Avenue
   New York NY 10016-2401
   Tel: 212-532-0800
   http://www.aftra.org

An association of university broadcasting faculty, industry professionals, and graduate students, BEA offers annual scholarships in broadcasting for college juniors, seniors, and graduate students. Visit its Web site for useful information about broadcast education and the broadcasting industry.
   Broadcast Education Association (BEA)
   1771 N Street, NW
   Washington, DC 20036-2891
   Tel: 202-429-3935
   http://www.beaweb.org

Contact the association for information on union membership.
National Association of Broadcast Employees and Technicians
501 Third Street, NW
Washington, DC 20001-2760
http://nabetcwa.org

The association provides information on broadcast education, scholarships for college students, jobs, and useful publications at its Web site.
National Association of Broadcasters
1771 N Street, NW
Washington, DC 20036-2800
Tel: 202-429-5300
E-mail: nab@nab.org
http://www.nab.org

Contact the association for information on farm broadcasting and membership, scholarships, and internships for college students.
National Association of Farm Broadcasting
700 Branch Street, Suite 8
PO Box 500
Platte City, MO 64079-0500
Tel: 816-431-4032
E-mail: info@nafb.com
http://nafb.com

Visit this organization's Web site to access scholarship and internship information (for college students), high school journalism resources and programs (such as the High School Broadcast Journalism Project), useful publications, and salary and employment surveys. The association also offers membership to college students.
Radio Television Digital News Association
529 14th Street, NW, Suite 425
Washington, DC 20045-1406
Tel: 202-659-6510
http://www.rtdna.org

Newspaper Editors

QUICK FACTS

School Subjects
English
Journalism

Personal Interests
Communication/ideas
Helping/teaching

Work Environment
Primarily indoors
Primarily one location

Minimum Education Level
Bachelor's degree

Salary Range
$28,430 to $58,580 to
$97,360+

Certification or Licensing
None available

Outlook
Little or no change

DOT
132

GOE
01.02.01

NOC
5122

O*NET-SOC
27-3041.00

OVERVIEW

Newspaper editors assign, review, edit, rewrite, and lay out all copy in a newspaper except advertisements. Editors sometimes write stories or editorials that offer opinions on issues. Editors review the editorial page and copy written by staff or syndicated columnists. A large metropolitan daily newspaper staff may include various editors who process thousands of words into print daily. A small town staff of a weekly newspaper, however, may include only one editor, who might be both owner and star reporter. Large metropolitan areas such as New York, Los Angeles, Chicago, and Washington, D.C., employ many editors. Approximately 61,110 editors are employed by newspaper, periodical, book, and directory publishers in the United States.

HISTORY

Journalism may have begun in 59 B.C. in Rome with the regular publication of reports called *Acta Diurna*, or *Daily Acts*. They reported political news and social events on a daily basis. In China, a journal called the *pao* was published on a regular basis from A.D. 618 until 1911, recording activities of the court. The first regularly printed European newspapers appeared in the early 1700s in Germany, The Netherlands, and Italy. The Dutch *corantos*, composed of items from the foreign press, were translated into English and French around 1620. The first English newspaper is considered to be the *Weekly Newes*, initially published in 1622. Until 1644, the news in English journals was controlled by the Star Chamber, a court that censored any unfavorable information about the king. Interestingly, also in

1644, the chamber was dismissed, and the English enjoyed the first semblance of freedom of the press. It was not until 1670 that the term "newspaper" came into use.

Benjamin Harris, an English journalist who immigrated to the United States, published the first American colonial newspaper in Boston in 1690, but because of the repressive climate of the times, it was immediately closed down by the British governor.

The first regularly circulated newspaper in the colonies was the *Boston News-Letter*, a weekly first published in 1704 by John Campbell. The press at this time still operated under rather severe government restrictions, but the struggle for freedom of the press grew, and before the end of the century, journalists were able to print the news without fear of repression.

The need for newspaper editors grew rapidly through the 19th and early 20th centuries as the demand for newspapers grew, causing circulation to jump from thousands to millions. New technology allowed the newspaper industry to meet the demand. Presses were invented that could produce newspapers by the millions on a daily basis.

In the 19th century, newspaper publishers began to endorse political candidates and to take stands on other political and social issues. They also came to be sources of entertainment. When Benjamin Day founded the *New York Sun* in 1833, he sought to do more than inform. The paper's pages were filled with news from the police beat as well as gossip, disasters, animal stories, and anecdotes. Other papers of the era began to print sports news, particularly horse racing and prizefights, society pages, and the business news from Wall Street. By the mid-19th century, there was an outpouring of human interest news, and journalists discovered the public appetite for scandal. By the end of the century, a number of newspaper editors were famed for their craft, including Horace Greeley of the *New York Tribune*, Charles A. Dana of the *New York Sun*, and William Allen White of the *Kansas Gazette*.

Newspaper sensationalism reached its peak during the last years of the 19th century and the first decades of the 20th. The most notable figure in this period of "yellow journalism" was William Randolph Hearst. He built a vast newspaper empire by playing on the emotions of his readership. Hearst often fabricated news, as did others, including his chief rival of the period, Joseph Pulitzer of the *New York World*. Perhaps the most glaring example of this type of journalism was Hearst and Pulitzer's exaggerated treatment of Spanish atrocities in Cuba, which incited public sentiment for war against Spain. Historians feel that the news coverage was at least partially responsible for the declaration of war that came in 1898. Although most newspapers through the 20th century have adhered to ethical journalistic practices, a number of dailies and weekly tabloids, protected by freedom of the press, continue to exploit the sensationalist market. Journalists in general, however, have adopted codes, such as that of the Society of Professional Journalists, which stress responsibility, freedom of the press, ethics, accuracy, objectivity, and fair play.

By the 20th century, newspapers became big business. Many newspaper publishing companies became corporate conglomerates that owned printing plants, radio and television stations, paper plants, forest acreage, and other related assets. Most of the profits came from advertising dollars as newspapers became the leading medium for advertising. As costs rose, it took more and more advertising to support the news portion of the paper, until advertising occupied most of the space in almost all U.S. newspapers. The amount of advertising, in most cases, now determines the amount of news coverage a newspaper carries. Eventually, many newspapers could not withstand the rising costs and the increased competition from television. From the mid-20th century newspapers started declining at a rapid rate. Between 1962 and 1990, for instance, the number of daily papers in the United States fell from 1,761 to 1,611.

As some papers failed, others, especially in large cities, grew as they took over new circulation. The major metropolitan dailies continued to add new and more exciting features in order to keep up with the competition, especially television.

From the beginning of the 20th century, newspapers had been expanding their coverage, and on large papers, editorial departments came to be divided into many specialty areas, requiring reporters and editors with equivalent specialties. Today, most newspapers have departments devoted to entertainment, sports, business, science, consumer affairs, education, and just about every other area of interest in today's society.

The economic recession, declining advertising revenue, and a decline in the number of newspaper subscribers has hit the newspaper industry hard in recent years. In fact, the number of daily newspapers in the United States decreased by nearly 13 percent from 1990 to 2008, according to the *Editor & Publisher International Yearbook*.

THE JOB

Newspaper editors are responsible for the paper's entire news content. The news section includes features, "hard" news, and editorial commentary. Editors of a daily paper's print edition plan the contents

Ben Bradlee (1921–)

One of the most influential figures in journalism today is Ben Bradlee. During his long career, he has served as a reporter, correspondent, managing editor, and executive editor, and has had a lasting influence on modern investigative journalism.

Benjamin Crowninshield Bradlee was born in Boston, Massachusetts, in 1921. He attended Harvard University, where he earned a bachelor's degree in 1942. After graduation he served in the navy during World War II. After the war, Bradlee began his long and illustrious career in journalism. His first job was as a reporter at *New Hampshire Sunday News*, which he began in 1946; he left in 1948 to serve as a reporter for the *Washington Post*, a morning daily newspaper published in Washington, D.C., and where he would eventually spend most of his career. In 1951 he moved to France to accept a position as press attaché to the U.S. Embassy in Paris. A few years later, he began working for *Newsweek*, first as a European correspondent based in Paris, then, in 1957, as a reporter based in Washington, D.C. He returned to the *Post* in 1965, assuming the position of managing editor. Three years later, he became vice president and executive editor of the newspaper, the latter position one that he would hold until 1991.

During Bradlee's time as executive editor of the *Post*, the newspaper won many Pulitzer Prizes. He is credited with turning the *Post* into one of the most important news publications in the world and for having a major influence on investigative journalism. Under his leadership, the *Post* was involved in two noteworthy examples of the power of investigative journalism and the importance of freedom of press. In 1971 the *Post* (along with the *New York Times*) challenged the U.S. federal government over the right to publish the controversial "Pentagon Papers," secret government documents detailing the role of the United States in Indochina (now Vietnam) from World War II to 1968. The newspapers won, scoring a huge victory for the concept of freedom of the press. The next year, two reporters from the *Post*, Bob Woodward and Carl Bernstein, tenaciously investigated a break-in at the Democratic National Party headquarters in the Watergate office complex and the ensuing scandal that implicated misconduct in the upper echelons of the White House. Their relentless pursuit of the facts—aided by "Deep Throat," their infamous anonymous source (in 2005, revealed to be W. Mark Felt, the deputy director of the FBI during the scandal)—contributed to the downfall of U.S. president Richard M. Nixon, who resigned in 1974.

Since retiring as executive editor in 1991 (he still serves as the *Post*'s vice-president at large), Bradlee has remained active in the field, speaking about such topics as ethics in journalism and pertinent issues in the industry. He published his memoir, *A Good Life*, in 1995.

Sources: PBS.org, Military.com, *A Good Life*

of each day's issue, assigning articles, reviewing submissions, prioritizing stories, checking wire services, selecting illustrations, and laying out each page with the advertising space allotted.

At a large daily newspaper, an *editor in chief* oversees the entire editorial operation, determines its editorial policy, and reports to the publisher. The *managing editor* is responsible for day-to-day operations in an administrative capacity. *Story editors*, or *wire editors*, determine which national news agency (or wire service) stories will be used and edit them. Wire services give smaller papers, without foreign correspondents, access to international stories.

A *city editor* gathers local and sometimes state and national news. The city editor hires copy editors and reporters, hands out assignments to reporters and photographers, reviews and edits stories, confers with executive editors on story content and space availability, and gives stories to copy editors for final editing.

A newspaper may have separate desks for state, national, and foreign news, each with its own head editor. Some papers have separate *editorial page editors*. The department editors oversee individual features; they *include business editors, fashion editors, sports editors, book section editors, entertainment editors*, and more. Department heads make decisions on coverage, recommend story ideas, and make assignments. They often have backgrounds in their department's subject matter and are highly skilled at writing and editing.

The copy desk, the story's last stop, is staffed by *copy editors*, who correct spelling, grammar, and punctuation mistakes; check for readability and sense; edit for clarification; examine stories for factual accuracy; and ensure the story conforms to editorial policy. Copy editors sometimes write headlines or picture captions and may crop photos. Occasionally they find serious problems that cause them to send stories back to the editors or the writer.

Editors, particularly copy editors, base many of their decisions on a stylebook that provides preferences in spelling, grammar, and word usage; it indicates when to use foreign spellings or English translations and the preferred system of transliteration. Some houses develop their own stylebooks, but often they use or adapt the *Associated Press Stylebook*.

After editors approve the story's organization, coverage, writing quality, and accuracy, they turn it over to the *news editors*, who supervise article placement and determine page layout with the advertising department. News and *executive editors* discuss the relative priorities of major news stories. If a paper is divided into several sections, each has its own priorities.

Photo editors are responsible for the look of final photographs to be published in a book or periodical or posted on the Internet. Some photo editors also work with video that is published online.

Modern newspaper editors depend heavily on computers. Generally, a reporter types the story directly onto the computer network, providing editors with immediate access. Some editorial departments are situated remotely from printing facilities, but computers allow the printer to receive copy immediately upon approval. Today, designers computerize page layout. Many columnists send their finished columns from home computers to the editorial department via modem or other electronic methods.

Most newspapers now have a presence on the Web; some are only available online. As newspaper publishers create online editions, *online editors* have come to play a crucial role at newspapers. This type of editor selects and updates online content (text, audio, video) as well as coordinates the graphic look of the pages. They are sometimes called *multimedia editors*. Online editors may be supervised by *online producers*. Online editors also work for television and radio stations that have a presence on the Web.

REQUIREMENTS

High School
English is the most important school subject for any future editor. You must have a strong grasp of the English language, including vocabulary, grammar, and punctuation, and you must be able to write well in various styles. Study journalism and take communications-related courses. Work as a writer or editor for your school paper or yearbook. Computer classes that teach word processing software and how to navigate the Internet will be invaluable in your future research. You absolutely must learn to type. If you cannot type accurately and rapidly, you will be at an extreme disadvantage.

Editors have knowledge in a wide range of topics, and the more you know about history, geography, math, the sciences, the arts, and culture, the better a writer and editor you will be.

Postsecondary Training
Look for a school with strong journalism and communications programs. Many programs require you to complete two years of liberal arts studies before concentrating on journalism studies. Journalism courses include reporting, writing, and editing; press law and ethics; journalism history; and photojournalism. Advanced classes include

Editors at the *Seattle Post-Intelligencer* participate in a news meeting. (*Ted S. Warren, AP Photo*)

feature writing, investigative reporting, and graphics. Some schools offer internships for credit.

When hiring, newspapers look closely at a candidate's extracurricular activities, putting special emphasis on internships, school newspaper and freelance writing and editing, and part-time newspaper work (stringing). Typing, computer skills, and knowledge of printing are helpful.

Other Requirements

To be a successful newspaper editor, you must have a love of learning, reading, and writing. You should enjoy the process of discovering information and presenting it to a wide audience in a complete, precise, and understandable way. You must be detail oriented and care about the finer points of accuracy, not only in writing, but also in reporting and presentation. You must be able to work well with coworkers, both giving and taking direction, and you must be able to work alone. Editors can spend long hours sitting at a desk in front of a computer screen.

EXPLORING

One of the best ways to explore this job is by working on your school's newspaper or other publication. You will most probably start as a staff writer or proofreader, but the experience will help you understand editing and how it relates to the entire field of publishing.

Keeping a journal is another good way to polish your writing skills and explore your interest in writing and editing your own work. In fact, any writing project will be helpful, since editing and writing are inextricably linked. Make an effort to write every day, even if it is only a few paragraphs. Try different kinds of writing, such as letters to the editor, short stories, poetry, essays, comedic prose, and plays.

EMPLOYERS

There are approximately 61,110 editors employed by newspaper, periodical, book, and directory publishers in the United States. Generally, newspaper editors are employed in every city or town, as many towns have at least one newspaper. As the population multiplies, so do the opportunities. In large metropolitan areas, there may be one or two daily papers, several general-interest weekly papers, ethnic and other special-interest newspapers, trade newspapers, and daily and weekly community and suburban newspapers. All of these publications need managing and department editors. Online papers also provide opportunities for editors.

Although many newspapers are privately owned or are owned by a small company or group of newspapers, there are several large newspaper companies that own many daily newspapers. These include Gannett Company Inc. (the publisher of *USA Today* and 83 other daily newspapers); the McClatchy Company (30 daily newspapers); Advance Publications Inc. (30 daily newspapers); New York Times Company (18 daily newspapers); Tribune Company (10 daily newspapers); and the Dow Jones & Company (eight daily newspapers, including the *Wall Street Journal).*

STARTING OUT

A typical route of entry into this field is by working as an *editorial assistant* or *proofreader.* Editorial assistants perform clerical tasks as well as some proofreading and other basic editorial tasks. Proofreaders can learn about editorial jobs while they work on a piece by looking at editors' comments on their work.

Job openings can be found using school career services offices, classified ads in newspapers and trade journals, and specialized publications such as *Publishers Weekly* (http://www.publishersweekly .com). Professional associations offer help-wanted sections or links to good job sites for editors and writers at their Web sites. The American Society of News Editors has links to job listings at its Web site, http://www.asne.org. In addition, many publishers have Web sites that list job openings. The following Web sites provide links to print journalism employers: JournalismJobs.com (http://www.journalism jobs.com), NewsLink (http://newslink.org), and Newspapers.com (http://www.newspapers.com).

ADVANCEMENT

Newspaper editors generally begin working on the copy desk, where they progress from less significant stories and projects to major news and feature stories. A common route to advancement is for copy editors to be promoted to a particular department, where they may move up the ranks to management positions. An editor who has achieved success in a department may become a city editor, who is responsible for news, or a managing editor, who runs the entire editorial operation of a newspaper.

EARNINGS

Salaries for newspaper editors vary from small to large communities, but editors generally are well compensated. Other factors affecting compensation include quality of education and previous experience, job level, and the newspaper's circulation. Large metropolitan dailies offer higher paying jobs, while outlying weekly papers pay less.

According to the U.S. Department of Labor, the mean annual income for newspaper, periodical, book, and directory editors was $58,580 in 2009. Salaries for all editors ranged from less than $28,430 to more than $97,360 annually.

On many newspapers, salary ranges and benefits, such as vacation time and health insurance, for most nonmanagerial editorial workers are negotiated by The Newspaper Guild.

WORK ENVIRONMENT

The environments in which editors work vary widely. For the most part, publishers of all kinds realize that a quiet atmosphere is conducive to work that requires tremendous concentration. It takes an unusual ability to edit in a noisy place. Most editors work in private offices or cubicles. Even in relatively quiet surroundings, however, editors often have many distractions.

Deadlines are an important issue for virtually all editors. Newspaper editors work in a much more pressured atmosphere than other editors because they face daily or weekly deadlines. To meet these deadlines, newspaper editors often work long hours. Some newspaper editors start work at 5:00 A.M., others work until 11:00 P.M. or even through the night. Those who work on weekly newspapers, including feature editors, columnists, and editorial page editors, usually work more regular hours.

OUTLOOK

Little or no employment change is expected for newspaper editors through 2018, according to the U.S. Department of Labor. In recent years, the newspaper industry has been hit hard be declining advertising revenues (revenue dropped by more than 25 percent from 2004 to 2008) and a declining number of subscribers. Some newspapers have even closed, while others have transitioned to publishing online only. As a result, there will be little if any employment growth for editors. Opportunities will be better on small daily and weekly newspapers, where the pay is lower. Some publications hire freelance editors to support reduced full-time staffs. And as experienced editors leave the workforce or move to other fields, job openings will occur. Opportunities will be best for editors with experience editing and producing content for electronic publication.

FOR MORE INFORMATION

For a list of accredited programs in journalism and mass communications, visit the ACEJMC Web site.

Accrediting Council on Education in Journalism and Mass Communications (ACEJMC)
University of Kansas School of Journalism and Mass Communications
Stauffer-Flint Hall, 1435 Jayhawk Boulevard
Lawrence, KS 66045-7575
Tel: 785-864-3973
http://www2.ku.edu/~acejmc/STUDENT/PROGLIST.SHTML

Visit the society's Web site for information on careers, job fairs, internships, high school journalism resources, diversity programs and to read A Career in Newspapers *and* Why Choose Journalism?: A Guide to Determining if a Career in Newspapers Is Right for You.
American Society of News Editors
11690B Sunrise Valley Drive
Reston, VA 20191-1409
Tel: 703-453-1122
http://www.asne.org

Visit the fund's Web site for information on print and online journalism careers, college and university journalism programs, high school journalism workshops, scholarships, internships, and job listings.

Dow Jones News Fund
PO Box 300
Princeton, NJ 08543-0300
Tel: 609-452-2820
E-mail: djnf@dowjones.com
https://www.newsfund.org

Visit this organization's Web site for information on investigative journalism and scholarships and membership for college students.

Investigative Reporters and Editors
Missouri School of Journalism
141 Neff Annex
Columbia, MO 65211-0001
Tel: 573-882-2042
E-mail: info@ire.org
http://www.ire.org

This nonprofit trade association represents the owners, publishers, and editors of community newspapers in the United States. Visit its Web site to read the Community Newspapers News and Notes blog.

National Newspaper Association
PO Box 7540
Columbia, MO 65205-7540
Tel: 800-829-4662
http://www.nnaweb.org

This trade association for African-American–owned newspapers has a foundation that offers a scholarship and internship program for inner-city high school juniors.

National Newspaper Publishers Association
http://www.nnpa.org

The nonprofit organization represents the $47 billion newspaper industry and more than 2,000 newspapers in the United States and Canada. Visit its Web site for information on trends in the industry and careers (including digital media job descriptions).

Newspaper Association of America
4401 Wilson Boulevard, Suite 900
Arlington, VA 22203-1867
Tel: 571-366-1000
http://www.naa.org

Visit the society's Web site for information on student chapters and scholarships for college students, job listings, training opportunities, educational resources, discussion boards and blogs, and much more.

Society of Professional Journalists
3909 North Meridian Street
Indianapolis, IN 46208-4011
Tel: 317-927-8000
http://www.spj.org

The SNA represents suburban and community newspapers in the United States and Canada. Visit its Web site for industry information.

Suburban Newspapers of America (SNA)
116 Cass Street
Traverse City, MI 49684-2505
Tel: 888-486-2466
E-mail: sna@suburban-news.org
http://www.suburban-news.org

Visit the following Web site for comprehensive information on journalism careers, summer programs, and college journalism programs:

High School Journalism
http://www.hsj.org

For comprehensive information for citizens, students, and news people about the field of journalism, visit

Project for Excellence in Journalism
1615 L Street, NW, Suite 700
Washington, DC 20036-5621
Tel: 202-419-3650
E-mail: mail@journalism.org
http://www.journalism.org

Online Producers

QUICK FACTS

School Subjects
Art
Computer science
English

Personal Skills
Helping/teaching
Leadership/management

Work Environment
Primarily indoors
Primarily one location

Minimum Education Level
Bachelor's degree

Salary Range
$28,430 to $59,710 to
$97,360+

Certification or Licensing
None available

Outlook
Faster than the average

DOT
131

GOE
01.02.01, 01.03.01

NOC
5123

O*NET-SOC
27-3022.00, 27-3041.00

OVERVIEW

Online producers organize and present information that is available on Web sites. They edit and/or write news stories, arrange the text, and any accompanying photos or videos for online publication. They sometimes collaborate with other workers to incorporate slideshows, animation, background music, or audio interviews to better complement a story. Some producers also create content for traditional broadcasts and print publications as part of their job duties. While many online producers are employed in journalism, a growing number of producers find work managing corporate Web sites for advertising agencies, employment firms, pharmaceutical companies, nonprofits, and other organizations. Online producers are also referred to as *multimedia producers, content producers*, and *online editors*.

HISTORY

The manner in which people receive news and other information has changed with the popularity of computers and access to the Internet. People crave news—from breaking stories to real-time baseball scores—and are no longer willing to wait until the next morning's edition of their favorite newspaper to stay up to speed with the world around them. Also, tablet computers and Smartphones have made access to the Internet possible as people go about their daily lives. Web-based editions of newspapers, television stations, magazines, and radio stations have quickly found an audience. Online producers, professionals with writing and editing skills, as well as computer savvy, are needed to maintain these sites with

Books to Read

Allan, Stuart. *Online News: Journalism and the Internet*. Maidenhead, U.K.: Open University Press, 2006.

Atton, Chris, and James F. Hamilton. *Alternative Journalism*. Sage Publications Ltd., 2008.

Boyd, Andrew. *Broadcast Journalism: Techniques of Radio and TV News*. St. Louis, Mo.: Focal Press, 2008.

Bull, Andy. *The NCTJ Essential Guide to Careers in Journalism*. Thousand Oaks, Calif.: Sage Publications Ltd., 2007.

Dominick, Joseph R., et al. *Broadcasting, Cable, the Internet and Beyond: An Introduction to Modern Electronic Media*. 6th ed. New York: McGraw-Hill, 2007.

Foust, James C. *Online Journalism: Principles and Practices of News for the Web*. 2d ed. Scottsdale, Ariz.: Holcomb Hathaway, Publishers, 2008.

Harrower, Tim. *Inside Reporting: A Practical Guide to the Craft of Journalism*. New York: McGraw-Hill Humanities/Social Sciences/Languages, 2006.

well-written and presented articles. Additionally, online producers are in demand in non-journalistic settings as many businesses and other organizations seek a place on the Internet.

THE JOB

Online producers working in journalism are responsible for the daily writing/editing and/or recording and presentation of information appearing on their organization's Web sites. Most forms of media—newspapers, magazines, television, and radio—have a Web-based equivalent where people can access news and information on a 24-hour basis. Online producers take news articles originally published in that day's paper or broadcast, and translate them into appropriate content for the organization's Web site. If new developments have occurred since the story was first printed, they are incorporated into the online version. They may also venture out of the newsroom and undertake reporting for new news stories. Some online producers may also write, record, and create content for traditional broadcasts and print versions of newspapers and other publications.

The Web version of a story must be presented in a different way than it is on paper—text is often edited to be more concise and engaging to the reader. The layout of the entire article is key—if it does not grab the reader's attention, the story may be ignored by online readers. Online producers often create and include features such as photos, video, audio, animation, music, or art. Since space is not an issue on the Web, many articles run with sidebars, photos, and other features not originally included in the print or broadcast edition. Online producers create special content packages such as videos or an audio slide show—a series of photos presented with an audio voiceover—to further enhance a story. Other stories lend themselves to special art provided by different vendors. Online producers, working with the advertising and technical departments, decide on which pieces to purchase and use. Sports sections, for example, oftentimes use team rosters and statistics to complement special event coverage such as the Super Bowl, the World Series, or the Olympic Games.

On an average shift, online producers can expect to produce about two to four dozen stories. Many of the stories are filtered from the day's print edition, but some will be reported directly from the field, or from newswire services. Some online producers, especially at smaller companies, are responsible for producing all news stories, regardless of subject. Online producers employed at large media companies may be assigned a specific beat or area of expertise such as world news or sports. Teamwork is part of the job as well. When an important story unfolds or a special edition is being created to cover a major event—such as the death of a religious leader or a presidential election—online producers will work with other members of the editorial staff to get the news posted as quickly as possible.

REQUIREMENTS

High School
Solid computer skills will give you the edge over other candidates. Prepare yourself by enrolling in every computer class your school has to offer, from programming to Web site design. Familiarize yourself with different software programs such as Adobe Photoshop, Avid NewsCutter, Final Cut Pro, and Adobe DreamWeaver, and different markup languages such as HTML. Round out your education with classes such as business, math, and English. Since many online producers have a journalism background, you will need strong reporting, writing, and editing skills to keep up with the competition. Any classes that require written reports as regular assignments are wise choices.

Postsecondary Training

While there are several routes of study to prepare for this career, many online producers enter the field after earning a bachelor's degree in journalism. In fact, many schools now offer Web-based media classes as an elective to their traditional journalism studies.

Other Requirements

Do you perform well under pressure? Can you quickly change gears and focus on a completely different project without complaining or losing momentum? Are you self-motivated and an independent worker, yet capable of being a team player? If you answer yes to these questions, you have some of the skills that are necessary for success in this industry.

EXPLORING

Creating your own Web site is an excellent way to explore this career. Not only will you gain experience in Web design, coding, and different software programs, you will have total editorial control.

Does your school paper have a Web site? If not, take the initiative and build one. As online producer for this project, you can add photo slideshows of the school prom, add a team roster graphic for the winning basketball team, and spice up your site with links to school clubs and organizations.

You should also surf the Web to view existing news and corporate Web sites. Write down what you like and dislike about each. Are the links relevant? Is the story portrayed in a concise, yet informative manner? If given the chance, what improvements would you make?

You might also consider becoming a student member of the Online News Association, a professional organization for online journalism professionals. Besides presenting the latest industry news, the association's Web site offers a wealth of information on available internships, school programs, conferences, and forums. Visit http://journalists.org/general/register_member_type.asp? for more information regarding a membership at the student level.

EMPLOYERS

Online producers work for newspapers, magazines, television and radio stations, advertising agencies, nonprofit organizations, government agencies, and any other company or organization that offers online content. Others are self-employed.

STARTING OUT

A job as an assistant or associate online producer is a common starting point for this career. Many companies hiring online producers require at least three years experience in Web journalism. Internships are your best bet to gain experience and training as well as valuable industry contacts for the future.

Check with local television stations, radio stations, and newspapers for available positions. Professional associations can also provide job leads. The Online News Association offers job listings for members (which include high school and college students) at its Web site, http://journalists.org. Poynter Online (http://www.poynter.org), besides being a great resource of industry news, offers seminars, fellowships, tip sheets, and links to employment possibilities.

ADVANCEMENT

Larger publications promote experienced online producers to senior or executive status. Those employed at regional publications could seek jobs at larger publications with broader news coverage.

EARNINGS

Although no specific salary statistics are available for online producers, earnings for these professionals are generally similar to that of traditional editors—although online editors may earn slightly more than their print counterparts. Salaries for all editors ranged from less than $28,430 to $97,360 or more in 2009, according to the U.S. Department of Labor. Editors who worked for newspaper, periodical, book, and directory publishers earned mean annual salaries of $58,580, while those employed in the radio and television broadcasting industries earned $56,200. Editors employed by other information services earned 59,710. Online producers typically receive benefits such as vacation and sick days and health insurance.

WORK ENVIRONMENT

Online producers—especially those in journalism—work in hectic, fast-paced environments. Deadlines are short and may come at any time. This means setting aside the current project, shifting gears, and quickly focusing on a breaking story. Online producers must be able to drop a story when necessary. Most online producers have more editorial control as opposed to editors on the print side of a publication. Since much of their work is done after editorial offices have closed for the day, they oftentimes make key decisions on what stories are posted at the organization's Web site.

Web sites operate 24 hours a day, seven days a week. News is often posted minutes after it has occurred. Work shifts are scheduled to accommodate this, and may vary from week to week. Nontraditional work hours can be physically exhausting and, at times, affect an online producer's personal life.

OUTLOOK

The Web has already had a major impact on how people receive and access their news and information. And with the popularity of laptop and tablet computers and Smartphones with Internet access, the number of people turning to Web-based news and information is expected to grow. Most, if not all, forms of traditional media—newspapers, magazines, radio, and television—have a Web-based counterpart. And with more corporate, small business, and professional organizations seeking a presence on the Web, the need for capable online producers is certain to increase.

Industry experts predict that some duties of online producers, such as story production and layout, may be eventually automated, leaving producers more time for original reporting in the field. Also, look for online producers to enjoy increasing opportunities with startup online publications that do not have ties to a print or broadcast entity.

FOR MORE INFORMATION

The Online News Association is a membership organization for journalists "whose principal livelihood involves gathering or producing news for digital presentation." Visit its Web site for information on membership for high school and college students.
Online News Association
http://journalists.org

Visit this organization's Web site to access scholarship and internship information (for college students), high school journalism resources and programs, useful publications, and salary and employment surveys. The association also offers membership to college students.
Radio Television Digital News Association
529 14th Street, NW, Suite 425
Washington, DC 20045-1406
Tel: 202-659-6510
http://www.rtdna.org

Photo Editors

QUICK FACTS

School Subjects
Art
Computer science
Journalism

Personal Skills
Artistic
Communication/ideas

Work Environment
Primarily indoors
Primarily one location

Minimum Education Level
Some postsecondary
training

Salary Range
$28,430 to $36,973 to
$57,642+

Certification or Licensing
None available

Outlook
About as fast as the average

DOT
143

GOE
N/A

NOC
5221

O*NET-SOC
27-3041.00, 27-4021.00

OVERVIEW

Photo editors are responsible for the look of final photographs to be published in a book or periodical or that appear electronically. Some photo editors also work with video. They make photo and video assignments, judge and alter pictures and video to meet assignment needs, and make sure all deadlines are met. Photo editors are also known as *picture editors* and *multimedia editors*.

HISTORY

For as long as photos have been in print, photo editors have been needed to evaluate them and delegate shooting assignments. In the early days of photography (the late 1800s), the jobs of photographer and editor were generally combined. On the staffs of early newspapers, it was not uncommon to have a story editor evaluate and place photos, or for a reporter to shoot his or her own accompanying photos as well as edit them for print. However, the need for a separate photo editor has become apparent as visual elements have become a larger part of print and online publications, advertisements, and even political campaigns. The trained eye and technical know-how of a photo editor is now an essential part of newsroom staffs and corporate offices everywhere.

As Internet journalism grows in popularity, photo editors are increasingly being asked to supervise videographers and prepare video for posting online.

THE JOB

The final look of a print or online publication is the result of many workers. The photo editor is responsible for the pictures, and often videos (electronic publishing), you see in these publications. They work with photographers, videographers, reporters, authors, copy editors, and company executives to make sure final photos help to illustrate, enlighten, or inspire the reader.

Photo editors, though knowledgeable in photography, generally leave the shooting to staff or contract photographers. Editors meet with their managers or clients to determine the needs of the project and brainstorm ideas for photos that will meet the project's goals. After picture ideas have been discussed, editors give photographers assignments, always including a firm deadline for completion. Most editors work for newspapers or magazines that face firm deadlines; if the editor does not have pictures to work with in time, the whole project is held up.

Once photos have arrived, the editor gets to work, using computer software to crop or enlarge shots, alter the coloring of images, or emphasize the photographer's use of shadows or light. All this work requires knowledge of photography, an aesthetic eye, and an awareness of the project's needs. Editors working for a newspaper must be sure to print or post photos that are true to life, while editors working for a fine-arts publication can alter images to create a more abstract effect.

Photo editors also purchase photographs from photo stock agencies to meet project needs. Depending on the size and type of company the editor works for, he or she might not have a staff of photographers to work with. Stock agencies fill this need. Editors can browse stock photos for sale online or in brochures. Even with purchased photos, the editor still has to make sure the image fits the needs and space of the project.

In addition to working with photos, editors have managerial tasks, such as assigning deadlines, organizing the office, ordering supplies, training employees, and overseeing the work of others. Along with copy and project editors, the photo editor is in contact with members of upper management or outside clients, and thus he or she is responsible for communicating their needs and desires with other workers.

REQUIREMENTS

High School

In addition to photography classes, take illustration and other art classes to develop an artistic eye and familiarize yourself with other forms of visual aids that are used in publications. Math classes will come in handy. To be able to determine what photo will meet the needs of a project, you will have to do a lot of reading, so English and communications classes are useful. Computer science classes will be invaluable. As an editor, you will work with computers almost daily and must be comfortable with art, layout, and word processing programs.

Postsecondary Training

While not required, most large and prestigious companies seek editors with a college degree in photography, visual art, or computer science. Employers will also want experience, so be sure to get as much exposure working on a publication as possible while in school. Other options are to go to a community college for a degree program; many offer programs in art or computer science that should be sufficient.

You should also be more than familiar with photo editing software such as Adobe Photoshop, Apple iPhoto, Corel Photo-Paint, Procreate Painter, and Jasc Paint Shop Pro, just to name a few.

Other Requirements

In addition to technical know-how, you should also be adept at working with people and for people. As an editor, you will often be the liaison between the client or upper management and the reporters and photographers working for you. You need to be able to communicate the needs of the project to all those working on it.

EXPLORING

To see if this career might be for you, explore your interests. Get involved with your school yearbook or newspaper. Both of these publications often appoint student photo editors to assist with photo acquisitions and layout. You should also try your hand at photography. To be a knowledgeable and successful editor, you need to know the medium in which you work.

You could also try to speak to a professional photo editor about his or her work. Ask a teacher or your counselor to set up a meeting, and think of questions to ask the editor ahead of time.

EMPLOYERS

Photo editors work for any organization that produces publications or online newsletters or has a Web site with many photos. This includes publishing houses, large corporations, Web site developers, nonprofit organizations, and the government. A large percentage of photo editors also work for stock photo agencies, either as staff photographers or as freelancers.

STARTING OUT

Photo editors often start out as photographers, staff writers, or other lower-level editors. They have to gain experience in their area of work, whether it is magazine publishing or Web site development, to be able to choose the right photos for their projects.

ADVANCEMENT

Photo editors advance by taking on more supervisory responsibility for their department or by working on larger projects for high-end clients. These positions generally command more money and can lead to chief editorial jobs. Freelance editors advance by working for more clients and charging more money for their services.

EARNINGS

Earnings for photo editors will vary depending on where they work. Payscale.com reports that in 2010, the median expected salary for a typical photo editor was approximately $36,973, but salaries ranged from less than $27,953 to more than $55,417. Salaries for Web photo editors ranged from less than $36,890 to $57,642 or more. Entry-level positions are often the same as those for other editorial positions, which is in the range of $28,430 or less. If the editor is employed by a corporation, stock photo agency, or other business, he or she typically will be entitled to health insurance, vacation time, and other benefits. Self-employed editors have to provide their own health and life insurance, but they can make their own schedules.

WORK ENVIRONMENT

Editors typically work in a comfortable office setting, with computers and other tools nearby. Depending on the workplace, the environment can be quiet and slow or busy with plenty of interruptions. Deadline pressures can make the job of photo editing hectic at times. Tight production schedules may leave editors with little time to acquire photos or assign work to photographers. Editors may have a quick turnaround time from when completed photos land on their desk to when the publication has to be sent to the printer. However, unless the editor works for a daily paper or weekly magazine, these busy periods are generally accompanied by slower periods with looser schedules. A good photo editor is flexible and able to work under both conditions.

OUTLOOK

Photo editing has been a popular and in-demand field for many years. Photo editors will be needed to help create a polished look to a print or online publication, such as a newspaper or magazine, selecting just the right photos to deliver the right message to readers. In the future, photo editors will increasingly be required to work with video and audio that is recorded by videographers. These multimedia recordings are used on newspaper and magazine Web sites, and in other settings.

FOR MORE INFORMATION

Visit the society's Web site for information about photojournalism, membership for college students, and the ASMP Bulletin.
American Society of Media Photographers (ASMP)
150 North Second Street
Philadelphia, PA 19106-1912
Tel: 215-451-2767
http://www.asmp.org

This organization provides workshops, conferences, and other professional meetings for "management or leadership-level people responsible for overseeing photography at their publications." Visit its Web site to read articles on news and developments within the industry.
Associated Press Photo Managers
450 West 33rd Street
New York, NY 10001-2603
E-mail: appm@ap.org
http://www.apphotomanagers.org

The association maintains a job bank, provides educational infor-mation, and makes insurance available to its members. It also pub-lishes News Photographer *magazine.*
National Press Photographers Association
3200 Croasdaile Drive, Suite 306
Durham, NC 27705-2588
Tel: 919-383-7246
http://www.nppa.org

The society is a group of amateur and professional photographers of all kinds offering information on exhibitions. It provides a forum for you to increase your knowledge, interact with others, and improve your photography.

Photographic Society of America
3000 United Founders Boulevard, Suite 103
Oklahoma City, OK 73112-4294
Tel: 405-843-1437
http://www.psa-photo.org

This organization provides training, publishes its own magazine, and offers various services for its members.

Professional Photographers of America
229 Peachtree Street, NE, Suite 2200
Atlanta, GA 30303-1608
Tel: 800-786-6277
http://www.ppa.com

══════ INTERVIEW ══════

John Klein is a photo editor at the Milwaukee Journal Sentinel. *He is currently the assignment editor for the photo department and the photo editor for the breaking news desk of JSOnline. John discussed his career with the editors of* Careers in Focus: Journalism.

Q. What made you want to enter this career?

A. I have worked as a photographer for newspapers since I was in high school. I liked the idea of being involved with people and events that made news. As a photojournalist every day is a new experience. The things I have seen and learned I could not get anywhere else. There is a certain element of excitement to covering news you cannot get just anywhere. I feel visual images need an advocate and that is a role I enjoy.

   As a photographer I had little control over how my work was used or what editors thought had strong visual impact. That led me to become a picture editor. I now have the opportunity to help lead a very talented group of photographers and have a real impact on how our publication uses visual images. I still have the excitement of working on big stories and meeting the constant deadlines of news photography.

   Now that more of my industry is moving toward the Internet, I have found a new outlet for photojournalism.

I have heard many photojournalists say doing this beats working for a living. Every day is new.

Q. Can you describe a typical day on the job?
A. My day begins at 6:00 A.M. I work the breaking news desk for JSOnline and am responsible for keeping fresh visual images on our Web site. I often shoot early morning photographs on my way to the office for fresh images online. We change our photographs several time over the course of the day so every time people go to our site there is something fresh for them to see.

Once in the office I make sure our Web site is updated, all photo requests are scheduled, and all our photographers have their daily assignments. It is up to me to be the gatekeeper for photo requests sent to our department. I often go to reporters and editors to talk about their request and visual needs. Next I begin to explore our visual needs for the news cycle, keeping in mind online as well as the daily paper. If there are stories that need photo coverage, I make the necessary arrangements or go to the reporter doing the story and talk to him or her about the story.

I sit next to the metro editor and the metro assignment editor and work very closely with them. It is ultimately my responsibility to see we have taken care of the visual needs of the paper. I also produce photo galleries for online. The rest of the day I am looking at future news and the photo budget, talking to reporters and editors, arranging photo coverage, and scheduling photographers.

Q. What are the pros and cons of work as a photo editor?
A. One of the biggest pros of working as a picture editor is having real input into our product. I am involved in the planning and execution of the paper and the Web site on a daily basis. Working for a news organization, I like being involved in the pace and deadlines of breaking stories and evolving news. I really enjoy editing the work of a very talented group of photographers as well as seeing photos that come in from news event around the world.

Being a former photographer I do miss being out on the street. While I get in on the action of following breaking stories I still, for the most part, remain in the office.

We do send picture editors to events from time to time. I enjoy being out of the office and coordinating teams of photographers covering news and sports events.

Being in the news business has afforded me the opportunity to cover celebrities, political figures, breaking news, and major sports.

Q. What are some of the most interesting or rewarding things that have happened to you while working as a photo editor?

A. As far as interesting: I have been involved in the coverage of several presidents, I have covered the Rose Bowl, I regularly cover Green Bay Packer games, and I am the go-to editor when it comes to breaking news. I have been the lead picture editor on several major projects. I have been involved in the creation of our Web site and seeing that it remains visually appealing. I really do have a window to what is happening in my community and the world.

As for rewarding: I get to see my efforts pay off instantly as I post photos or build galleries on our Web site. I see my efforts every day in the newspaper. I get to see the results of my work every time a photographer comes back with a great picture. I see my name in the paper or online if a byline is given. I do hear from our readers if they like what we are doing. The biggest thrill for me is seeing my work in print or online.

Q. What is the employment outlook for photo editors?

A. I am afraid the outlook for newspapers and magazines is not good. Fewer and fewer people are reading printed publications. Online publications are growing every day. We get thousands of hits every day on our Web site, and photos are one of the biggest draws. People will flock to our photo galleries when there is a big event. I feel there will always be a need for news gatherers and editors and more so as the Internet grows.

One new area of visual editing is in multimedia. This is a new avenue for visual editors. While much of the technology is new and different, the basic skills are the same—a sense of what makes good visuals and news judgment. We are now creating and editing videos, audio slide shows, and photo galleries. I think there will always be a need for good visual editors to help maintain high visual standards.

Photographers and Photojournalists

OVERVIEW

Photographers take and sometimes develop and print pictures of people, places, objects, and events, using a variety of cameras and photographic equipment. They work in the publishing, advertising, public relations, science, and business industries, as well as provide personal photographic services. They may also work as fine artists.

Photojournalists, also called *news photographers*, shoot photographs that capture news events. Their job is to tell a story with pictures. They may cover a war in central Africa, the Olympics, a national election, or a small town's Fourth of July parade. In addition to shooting pictures, photojournalists also write captions or other supporting text to provide further detail about each photograph. Photojournalists may also develop and print photographs or edit digital photographs. There are approximately 152,000 photographers and photojournalists employed in all industries the United States.

HISTORY

The word *photograph* means "to write with light." Although the art of photography goes back only about 150 years, the two Greek words that were chosen and combined to refer to this skill quite accurately describe what it does.

The discoveries that led eventually to photography began early in the 18th century when a German scientist, Dr. Johann H. Schultze, experimented with the action of light on certain chemicals. He found that when these chemicals were covered by dark paper they did not change color, but when they were exposed to sunlight, they darkened. A French painter named Louis Daguerre became the first photographer in 1839, using silver-iodide-coated plates and a small box. To develop images on the plates, Daguerre exposed them to mercury vapor. The daguerreotype, as these early photographs came to be known, took minutes to expose and the developing process was directly to the plate. There were no prints made.

Although the daguerreotype was the sensation of its day, it was not until George Eastman invented a simple camera and flexible roll film that photography began to come into widespread use in the late 1800s. After exposing this film to light and developing it with chemicals, the film revealed a color-reversed image, which is called a negative. To make the negative positive (in other words, to print a picture), light must be shone though the negative onto light-sensitive paper. This process can be repeated to make multiple copies of an image from one negative.

Photojournalism started in the early 1920s with the development of new camera equipment that could be easily transported as news occurred. A growing market for photographically illustrated magazines revealed a population wanting news told through pictures and also reflected a relatively low level of literacy among the general public. As World Wars I and II ravaged Europe and the rest of the world, reporters were either handed a camera or were accompanied by photographers to capture the gruesome and sometimes inspirational images of courage during combat.

In 1936, *Life* magazine was launched and quickly became one of the most popular vehicles for the photo essay, a news piece consisting mainly of photographs and their accompanying captions. Soon, however, photojournalists left the illustrated magazine market for news organizations catering to the larger newspapers and television networks. Less emphasis was placed on the photo essay; instead, photojournalists were more often asked to track celebrities or gather photos for newspaper advertising.

One of the most important developments in recent years is digital photography. In digital photography, instead of using film, pictures are recorded on microchips, which can then be downloaded onto a computer's hard drive. They can be manipulated in size, color, and shape, virtually eliminating the need for a darkroom.

Digital photography has also affected the field of photojournalism. Many papers have pared down their photography staff and purchase stock photos from photo agencies. Some smaller papers might even hand staff reporters digital cameras to illustrate their own

Photojournalists photograph a news conference outside a courthouse.
(Jeff Greenberg, Photo Edit)

stories. Still, photojournalists have a place in the working world, as their trained "eyes" for perfect shots will always be in demand.

THE JOB

Photography is both an artistic and technical occupation. There are many variables in the process that a knowledgeable photographer can manipulate to produce a clear image or a more abstract work of fine art. First, all photographers (including photojournalists) know how to use cameras and can adjust focus, shutter speeds, aperture, lenses, and filters. They know about the types and speeds of films (if they still use traditional cameras). Photographers also know about light and shadow, deciding when to use available natural light and when to set up artificial lighting to achieve desired effects.

Some photographers still send their film to laboratories, but others develop their own negatives and make their own prints. These processes require knowledge about chemicals such as developers and fixers and how to use enlarging equipment. Photographers must also be familiar with the large variety of papers available for printing photographs, all of which deliver a different effect. Most photographers continually experiment with photographic processes to improve their technical proficiency or to create special effects.

More often than not, photojournalists use digital cameras to eliminate the need for developing film. Since the debut of the first digital camera designed for newspapers in the early 1990s, digital photography has revolutionized photojournalism. Unlike traditional film cameras, digital cameras use electronic memory rather than a negative to record an image. The image can then be downloaded instantly into a computer and sent worldwide via e-mail or by posting it on the Internet. By eliminating developing and transportation time, digital cameras allow a sports photographer to shoot a picture of the game-winning basket and immediately transmit it to a newspaper hundreds of miles away before a late-night deadline.

Photographers usually specialize in one of several areas: portraiture, commercial and advertising photography, fine art, educational photography, or scientific photography. There are subspecialties within each of these categories. A *scientific photographer*, for example, may specialize in aerial or underwater photography. A *commercial photographer* may specialize in food or fashion photography.

Another popular specialty for photographers is photojournalism. Photojournalists are photographers who capture stories of everyday life or news events that, supported with words, tell stories to the entire world or to the smallest of communities. Photojournalists are the eyes of the community, allowing viewers to be a part of events that they would otherwise not have access to.

Actually shooting the photographs is just a portion of the photojournalist's job. They also write the cutlines or captions that go with each photograph and prepare the digital images using computer software for publication. For large photo-essay assignments, they research the subject matter and supervise the layout of the pages.

Technology continues to change the work of photojournalists. In addition to taking photographs, photojournalists are increasingly being asked to shoot video that can be used on Web sites, newscasts, and in other settings. Dirck Halstead, editor and publisher of *The Digital Journalist* online magazine, says that newspapers and magazines are equipping their photojournalists with high-definition video cameras that allow them to take video that can be used on their Web sites and also as high-definition screen captures on the front pages of their print editions.

Some photojournalists work on the staffs of weekly or daily newspapers, while others take photographs for magazines or specialty journals. Most magazines employ only a few or no photographic staff, but depend on freelance photojournalists to provide their pictures. *Magazine photojournalists* sometimes specialize in a specific field, such as sports or food photography.

Some photographers and photojournalists write for trade and technical journals, teach photography in schools and colleges, act as representatives of photographic equipment manufacturers, sell photographic equipment and supplies, produce documentary films, or do freelance work.

REQUIREMENTS

High School

While in high school, take as many art classes and photography classes as are available. Chemistry is useful for understanding developing and printing processes (if you plan to use a traditional camera in your work). You can learn about photo editing software and digital photography in computer classes, and business classes will help if you are considering a freelance career.

If you decide to specialize in photojournalism, you will need a well-rounded education. Take classes in English, foreign language, history, and the sciences to prepare yourself for the job.

Postsecondary Training

Although some colleges and universities offer photojournalism majors, many offer a journalism major with three to four photography courses. A journalism degree is not a prerequisite to becoming a photojournalist, although college training probably offers the most promising assurance of success in fields such as industrial, news, or scientific photography. There are degree programs at the associate's, bachelor's, and master's levels. Many men and women, however, become photographers with no formal education beyond high school.

Many journalism programs require their students to complete internships with newspapers or other local employers. This is essential to building your experience and getting a good job in this competitive field. Many photojournalists are offered their first jobs directly from their internship experience.

Other Requirements

You should possess manual dexterity, good eyesight and color vision, and artistic ability to succeed in this line of work. You need an eye for form and line, an appreciation of light and shadow, and the ability to use imaginative and creative approaches to photographs, especially in commercial work. In addition, you should be patient and accurate and enjoy working with detail.

Self-employed (or freelance) photographers need good business skills. They must be able to manage their own studios, including hiring and managing assistants and other employees, keeping records, and maintaining photographic and business files. Marketing and sales skills are also important to a successful freelance photography business.

Because of the timely nature of many assignments, photojournalists must be able to work under the pressures of a deadline. They may be assigned to shoot pictures of people in trying situations, such as house fires, car wrecks, or military combat. In these cases, the photojournalist must be extremely sensitive to the people at the center of the story, ask permission to take photos, and when possible, ask for details about what happened. To do this, photojournalists must be extremely tactful and polite and work well under stress.

EXPLORING

Photography is a field that anyone with a camera can explore. To learn more about this career, you can join high school camera clubs, yearbook or newspaper staffs, photography contests, and community hobby groups. You can also seek a part-time or summer job in a camera shop. Other good ways to learn more about the field include reading books and magazines about photography/photojournalism and talking to a professional about his or her career.

EMPLOYERS

About 152,000 photographers and photojournalists work in the United States, more than half of who are self-employed. About 10 percent of photographers are employed by newspaper, periodical, book, and directory publishers. Most jobs for photographers are provided by photographic or commercial art studios; other employers include newspapers and magazines, radio and TV broadcasting, government agencies, and manufacturing firms. Colleges, universities, and other educational institutions employ photographers to prepare promotional and educational materials.

A large percentage of photojournalists work as freelance contractors. Photo agencies and news organizations such as the Associated Press purchase photos from freelance photojournalists to use in print and online publications. Some photojournalists work on staff for newspapers, magazines, or other print publications. Television networks also hire photojournalists to help illustrate breaking stories.

STARTING OUT

Some photographers enter the field as apprentices, trainees, or assistants. Trainees may work in a darkroom, camera shop, or developing laboratory. They may move lights and arrange backgrounds for a commercial or portrait photographer. Assistants spend many months learning this kind of work before they move into a job behind a camera.

Many photojournalists get their first jobs through an internship or contact at a local paper. The National Press Photographers Association offers a job bank at its Web site, http://www.nppa.org. Print and online classified advertisements are another way to find out about job openings.

Many large cities offer schools of photography, which may be a good way to start in the field. Beginning photojournalists may work for one of the many newspapers and magazines published in their area. Other photographers choose to go into business for themselves as soon as they have finished their formal education. Setting up a studio may not require a large capital outlay, but beginners may find that success does not come easily.

ADVANCEMENT

Because photography is such a diversified field, there is no usual way in which to get ahead. Those who begin by working for someone else may advance to owning their own businesses. Commercial photographers may gain prestige as more of their pictures are placed in well-known trade journals or popular magazines. Photojournalists can advance by shooting for more prestigious papers (and earning more money for it) or by going into business on their own. They can advance to become the *head photo editor*, in charge of a staff of photojournalists, or they can even become managing editors or editors in chief of a publication. Other newspaper photojournalists move into magazine photography, usually on a freelance basis. Where newspaper photojournalists are generalists, magazine photography is usually more specific in nature. A few photographers may become celebrities in their own right by making contributions to the art world or the sciences.

EARNINGS

The U.S. Department of Labor reports that salaried photographers had median annual earnings of $29,770 in 2009. Salaries ranged from less than $17,120 to more than $62,340. Mean annual earnings for photographers employed in newspaper, periodical, book, and directory publishers were $42,430 in 2009. Those who worked in radio and television broadcasting earned $42,810.

Self-employed photographers often earn more than salaried photographers, but their earnings depend on general business conditions.

In addition, self-employed photographers do not receive the benefits that a company provides its employees.

Photographers in salaried jobs usually receive benefits such as paid holidays, vacations, sick leave, and medical insurance.

WORK ENVIRONMENT

Work conditions vary based on the job and employer. Many photographers work a 35- to 40-hour workweek, but freelancers and news photographers often put in long, irregular hours. Commercial and portrait photographers work in comfortable surroundings. Photojournalists seldom are assured physical comfort in their work and may in fact face danger when covering stories on natural disasters or military conflicts. Some photographers work in research laboratory settings; others work on aircraft; and still others work underwater. For some photographers, conditions change from day to day. One day, they may be photographing a hot and dusty rodeo; the next they may be taking pictures of a dog sled race in Alaska.

In general, photographers work under pressure to meet deadlines and satisfy customers. Freelance photographers have the added pressure of uncertain incomes and have to continually seek out new clients.

For freelance photographers, the cost of equipment can be quite expensive, with no assurance that the money spent will be repaid through income from future assignments. Freelancers in travel-related photography, such as travel and tourism photographers and photojournalists, have the added cost of transportation and accommodations. For all photographers, flexibility is a major asset.

OUTLOOK

Employment of photographers and photojournalists will increase about as fast as the average for all occupations through 2018, according to the *Occupational Outlook Handbook*. The demand for new images should remain strong in education, communication, entertainment, marketing, and research. As the Internet grows and more newspapers and magazines turn to electronic publishing, demand will increase for photographers to produce digital images. If the newspaper and magazine industries continue to contract, there will be fewer opportunities for photojournalists.

Photography is a highly competitive field. There are far more photographers and photojournalists than positions available. Only those who are extremely talented and highly skilled can support themselves as self-employed workers in these professions. Many photographers and photojournalists take pictures as a sideline while working another job.

Knowledge of new technology (especially digital and video cameras) and the existing art form of photography is essential. Excellent people and marketing skills will give you an edge for photojournalism positions.

FOR MORE INFORMATION

Visit the society's Web site for information about photojournalism, membership for college students, and the ASMP Bulletin.

American Society of Media Photographers (ASMP)
150 North Second Street
Philadelphia, PA 19106-1912
Tel: 215-451-2767
http://www.asmp.org

The association maintains a job bank, provides educational information, and makes insurance available to its members. It also publishes News Photographer *magazine.*

National Press Photographers Association
3200 Croasdaile Drive, Suite 306
Durham, NC 27705-2588
Tel: 919-383-7246
E-mail: info@nppa.org
http://www.nppa.org

The society is a group of amateur and professional photographers of all kinds offering information on exhibitions. It provides a forum for you to increase your knowledge, interact with others, and improve your photography.

Photographic Society of America
3000 United Founders Boulevard, Suite 103
Oklahoma City, OK 73112-4294
Tel: 405-843-1437
http://www.psa-photo.org

This organization provides training, publishes its own magazine, and offers various services for its members.

Professional Photographers of America
229 Peachtree Street, NE, Suite 2200
Atlanta, GA 30303-1608
Tel: 800-786-6277
http://www.ppa.com

For information on student membership, contact
Student Photographic Society
229 Peachtree Street, NE, Suite 2200
Atlanta, GA 30303-1608
Tel: 866-886-5325
E-mail: info@studentphoto.com
http://www.studentphoto.com

INTERVIEW

Stacey Wescott is a photojournalist for the Chicago Tribune. *She discussed her career with the editors of* Careers in Focus: Journalism.

Q. What made you want to enter this career?

A. I fell in love with photography in the darkroom. I remember being mesmerized by the images as they developed on the paper in the huge trays of photo chemicals. I spent hours and hours in the dark room. I loved the lack of light, the smell, the quietness, and the intimacy of just me and my pictures. Looking back, I think it was truly that I was discovering a part of myself in the images developing on the paper. Each image that I made then, and make now as a photographer, says as much about me as it says about my subject. Initially, I started taking my photography classes in the studio arts department, but later switched to the journalism school when I realized that it had more practical uses that could directly influence the world around me.

I was not the kind of kid who read *National Geographic* and wanted to travel to exotic places and take pictures. Instead, I grew up a park rat. I spent every day playing sports, any sport. I was always moving and I was very competitive (which comes from being raised in a family of five kids). Additionally, I am a product of a family very involved in social justice and truth-seeking. Both my parents are outspoken and very much about the "underdog." In college at the University of Minnesota, I was very politically active, especially as it related to U.S. intervention in Latin America and the university's investments in South Africa (apartheid). I saw photography as a vehicle to documenting the protests that I was participating in. I felt it was a way to keep better tabs on the police intervening in these protests and make sure that they were not abusing their power. I also thought it was important to have documentation for when I traveled abroad. I wanted people in Latin America to know that not all Americans were apathetic and on-board with the Ronald Reagan politics of the 1980s era. In the late 80s and early 90s, I ended up spending three and a half years living in Latin America (Colombia and Uruguay) and again I utilized my photography, documenting the political struggles of students in Bogotá, Colombia. At that time I wasn't much of a newspaper photographer as I had never worked for my college newspaper. Instead [I used photography] to support whatever projects I was working on—student protests, women artists, exhibits, etc.

I fell in love with photography for lots of reasons, but what made me want to enter this career in1997 was that I finally realized that I had a true affinity with photography: time disappeared, work never felt like work, it allowed me a lot of autonomy, and doors started to open.

Q. Can you describe a typical day on the job?

A. I am both a photographer and a hybrid editor of sorts. I work eight to 12 hours, depending on what is on my plate. We have 23 photographers on staff at the *Tribune*, each with a different shift. My shift is from 9 to 5, though I am usually doing computer/phone work from 6 to 7:30 A.M. Here are some of my main duties:

- I check Web sites and listen to the radio to learn about overnight news.
- I check, recharge, and gather my equipment.
- I talk with the assignment editor on the photo desk and to the bureau chief for the zone I cover.
- I check for new photo assignments and developing stories in the NewsGate system. Then I assign the work to myself, freelancers, or other staff photographers working in my zone.
- I travel to assignments, shoot them, and transmit the photos.
- I am constantly adjusting my schedule depending on what news is breaking or last-minute assignments are coming in.
- I also look for stories to pitch to my editors. On average I pitch one to two cover stories a month.

In addition to my work duties, I also balance (along with my husband) taking care of our two daughters, ages five and eight.

Q. What are some of the pros and cons of work as a photojournalist?

A. PROS: I think of this job as a blessing and a gift. I love what I do. I love the creativity involved in shooting. I love the constant and continuous movement within the community. I love learning about other people's lives and what makes them tick. I also love the autonomy of what I do. Though I am in constant communication with editors, I basically do my job alone. I get to live within my own thoughts and ideas most of the time, and there are endless possibilities to the photos and stories I can work on.

CONS: The job can be exhausting both mentally and physically as photographers and photo editors have to keep pace with breaking news, daily stories, and long-term projects. We are also expected to learn new software systems as they are implemented in the newsroom and learn about new equipment as our cameras are updated. Additionally, a strong knowledge of multimedia/video has become an important component of photojournalism over the last five years.

Q. What advice would you give to young people who want to enter this field?

A. If you are lazy and don't want to work long days, find a different job. You have to work harder and longer than anyone else—the best light is early and late in the day, expect to capture both times of day. You have to be self-motivated. You have to be humble. You have to pay your dues. Don't complain, don't ever turn down work, and be prepared to make something out of a nothing assignment. If you have a girlfriend or boyfriend who doesn't understand the demands of this job, be prepared to let them go. Be well trained in multimedia as well as still photography. Be prepared to live anywhere the job takes you. This job is what you make of it.

Q. What is one of the most interesting or rewarding things that has happened to you while working as a photojournalist?

A. This question could be answered in 100 different ways. The most personally rewarding thing that has resulted from my work as a photojournalist is that I have been able to bring faith and spirituality back into my life. I have worked every Sunday for the last 10 years so I have had the privilege of having assignments at all sorts of places of worship. Being exposed to all of these different faiths has been eye opening and rejuvenating. I still don't know exactly how to define this, but I know that embracing faith and praying every day is important. It helps me count my blessings, keep life in perspective, and treat others with respect and dignity.

Prepress Workers

QUICK FACTS

School Subjects
Computer science
Mathematics
Technical/shop

Personal Skills
Artistic
Technical/scientific

Work Environment
Primarily indoors
Primarily one location

Minimum Education Level
Some postsecondary training

Salary Range
$21,610 to $35,810 to
$55,770

Certification or Licensing
None available

Outlook
Decline

DOT
979

GOE
08.03.05

NOC
9472

O*NET-SOC
51-5021.00, 51-5022.00,
51-5022.01, 51-5022.02,
51-5022.03, 51-5022.04,
51-5022.05, 51-5022.06,
51-5022.07, 51-5022.08

OVERVIEW

Prepress workers handle the first stage in the printing process. This initial phase of production involves multiple steps, including managing electronic files submitted by customers and, for some print jobs, making printing plates.

According to the U.S. Department of Labor (DOL), 106,900 people are employed as prepress workers. Many of these jobs are with commercial printing companies. Other jobs are with prepress service bureaus (companies that deal exclusively with prepress work) and newspapers and magazines.

HISTORY

The history of modern printing began with the invention of movable type in the 15th century. For several centuries before that, books had been printed from carved wooden blocks or laboriously copied by hand. These painstaking methods of production were so expensive that books were chained to prevent theft.

In the 1440s, Johannes Gutenberg invented a form of metal type that could be used over and over. The first known book to be printed with this movable type was a Bible in 1455—the now-famous Gutenberg Bible. Gutenberg's revolutionary new type greatly reduced the time and cost involved in printing, and books soon became plentiful.

Ottmar Mergenthaler, a German immigrant to the United States, invented the Linotype machine in 1886. Linotype allowed the typesetter to set type from a keyboard that used a mechanical device to set letters in place. Before this, printers were setting type by hand, one letter at a time, picking up each letter individually from their typecases as they had been doing for more than 400 years. At about the same time, Tolbert Lanston invented the Monotype machine, which also had a keyboard but set the type as individual letters. These inventions allowed compositors to set type much faster and more efficiently.

With these machines, newspapers advanced from the small two-page weeklies of the 1700s to the huge editions of today's metropolitan dailies. The volume of other periodicals, advertisements, books, and other printed matter also proliferated.

In the 1950s, a new system called photocomposition was introduced into commercial typesetting operations. In this system, typesetting machines used photographic images of letters, which were projected onto a photosensitive surface to compose pages. Instructions to the typesetting machine about which letters to project and where to project them were fed in through a punched-paper or magnetic tape, which was, in turn, created by an operator at a keyboard.

Most recently, typesetting has come into the home and office in the form of desktop publishing. This process has revolutionized the industry by enabling companies and individuals to do their own type composition and graphic design work. With the introduction of desktop publishing and other computer technology, the prepress process has changed dramatically over the past decade. Computerized processes have replaced many of the traditional processes, eliminating a number of prepress jobs but opening up new opportunities as well.

THE JOB

Prepress work involves a variety of tasks, most of which are now computer-based. In commercial printing plants, jobs tend to come from customers on computer disk or via a file transfer protocol Web site.

The electronic file is reviewed by the *preflight technician* to ensure that all of its elements are properly formatted and set up. At small print shops—which account for the majority of the printing industry—a *job printer* is often the person in charge of proofing the file, fixing any problems that emerge, and taking the job to the printing stage.

Once a file is ready, the technician transmits it through an image-setter onto paper, film, or directly to the printing plate. The latter method is called digital imaging, and it bypasses the film stage altogether. Direct-to-plate technology has been adopted by many printing companies nationwide. When direct-to-plate technology is used, the prepress technician creates an electronic image of the printed pages. The image is then converted into a proof that is e-mailed or mailed to the customer for review, corrections, and eventual approval for printing. Once the job is approved, prepress workers use laser technology to transfer the images directly to the metal plates or directly to a digital press that will be used to print the job.

REQUIREMENTS

Educational requirements for prepress workers vary according to the area of responsibility, but all require at least a high school diploma, and most call for a strong command of computers.

Whereas prepress areas used to be typesetting and hand-composition operations run by people skilled in particular crafts, they are now predominantly computer-based. Workers are no longer quite as specialized and generally are competent in a variety of tasks. Thus, one of the most important criteria for prepress workers today is a solid base of computer knowledge, ideally in programs and processes related to graphic design and prepress work.

High School

Young people interested in the field are advised to take courses in computer science, mathematics, and electronics.

Postsecondary Training

Postsecondary education is strongly encouraged for most prepress positions and a requirement for some jobs, including any managerial role. Graphic arts programs are offered by community and junior colleges as well as four-year colleges and universities. Postsecondary programs in printing technology are also available.

Any programs or courses that give you exposure to the printing field will be an asset. Courses in printing and printing-related computer software and other technologies are often available at vocational-technical institutes and through printing trade associations.

Other Requirements

Prepress work requires strong communication skills, attention to detail, and the ability to perform well in a high-pressure, deadline-driven environment. Physically, you should have good manual dexterity, good eyesight, and good overall visual perception. Artistic skill is an advantage in nearly any prepress job. Computer skills are increasingly important as technology plays a more integral role in the printing industry.

EXPLORING

A summer job or internship doing basic word processing or desktop publishing is one way to get a feel for what prepress work involves. Such an opportunity could even be found through a temporary agency. Of course, you will need a knowledge of computers and certain software.

You also can volunteer to do desktop publishing or design work for your school newspaper or yearbook. This would have the added benefit of exposing you to the actual printing process.

EMPLOYERS

Approximately 106,900 people are employed as prepress workers in the United States. Most prepress work is in firms that do commercial or business printing and in newspaper plants. Other jobs are at companies that specialize in certain aspects of the prepress process, for example, platemaking or outputting of film.

Because printing is so widespread, prepress jobs are available in almost any part of the country. However, according to the *Occupational Outlook Handbook*, prepress work is concentrated in large printing centers like New York, Chicago, Los Angeles, Philadelphia, Los Angeles-Long Beach, Minneapolis-St. Paul, Boston, and Washington, D.C.

STARTING OUT

Information on apprenticeships and training opportunities is available through state employment services and local chapters of printing industry associations.

If you wish to start working first and learn your skills on the job, you should contact potential employers directly, especially if you want to work in a small nonunion print shop. Openings for trainee positions may be listed in newspaper want ads or with the state employment service. Trade school graduates may find jobs through their school's career services office. And industry association offices often run job-listing services.

ADVANCEMENT

Workers often begin as assistants and move into on-the-job training programs. Entry-level workers are trained by more experienced workers and advance according to how quickly they learn and prove themselves.

In larger companies, prepress workers can move up the ranks to take on supervisory roles. Prepress and production work is also a good starting point for people who aim to become a customer service or sales representative for a printing company.

EARNINGS

Pay rates vary for prepress workers, depending on their level of experience and responsibility, type of company, where they live, and whether they are union members. Prepress workers had median annual earnings of $35,810 in 2009, according to the DOL. Salaries ranged from less than $21,610 to $55,770 or more. Mean earnings in printing and related support activities, the industry employing the largest number of prepress technicians and workers, were $37,880.

According to the *Printing Industries of America Compensation Report 2008*, electronic prepress technicians earned median annual salaries of $39,936. The most experienced technicians earned $77,376.

Median annual salaries for job printers were $34,440 in 2009, according to the DOL. Salaries ranged from less than $21,350 to $53,250 or more.

Benefits for full-time workers include vacation and sick time, health, and sometimes dental, insurance, and pension or 401(k) plans.

WORK ENVIRONMENT

Generally, prepress workers work in clean, quiet settings away from the noise and activity of the pressroom. Prepress areas are usually air-conditioned and roomy. Preflight technicians and others who work in front of computer terminals can risk straining their eyes, as well as their backs and necks.

An eight-hour day is typical for most prepress jobs, but frequently workers put in more than eight hours. Prepress jobs at newspapers and financial printers often call for weekend and evening hours.

OUTLOOK

Employment for prepress workers is expected to decline rapidly through 2018, according to the DOL. While it is anticipated that the demand for printed materials will increase, prepress work will not, mainly because of new innovations and technology that allow prepress workers to do their jobs more efficiently. Despite this prediction, the DOL reports that there should continue to be good opportunities for prepress workers with "good computer and customer service skills." Specialized computer skills will increasingly be needed to handle direct-to-plate and other new technology.

Given the increasing demand for rush print jobs, printing trade service companies should offer good opportunities for prepress workers. Larger companies and companies not equipped for specialized prepress work will continue to turn to these specialty shops to keep up with their workload.

FOR MORE INFORMATION

This trade association represents trade binders, loose-leaf manufacturers, and suppliers throughout the United States, Canada, and Europe. For industry news and other resources, contact
Binding Industries Association
200 Deer Run Road
Sewickley, PA 15143-2324
Tel: 800-910-4283
E-mail: printing@printing.org
http://www.printing.org/node/3678

This union represents U.S. and Canadian workers in all craft and skill areas of the printing and publishing industries. For information on education and training programs available through local union schools, contact
Graphic Communications Conference of the International
   Brotherhood of Teamsters
25 Louisiana Avenue, NW
Washington, DC 20001-2130
Tel: 202-624-6800
http://www.teamster.org/content/graphics-communications

This trade association of graphic communications and graphic arts supplier companies offers economic and management information, publications, and industry reports and studies.
IPA—The Association of Graphic Solutions Providers
7200 France Avenue South, Suite 223
Edina, MN 55435-4309
Tel: 800-255-8141
http://www.ipa.org

This graphic arts trade association is a good source of general information about the printing industry.
NAPL
75 West Century Road, Suite 100
Paramus, NJ 07652-1461
Tel: 800-642-6275
http://public.napl.org

This coalition serves as a clearinghouse, resource center, and coordinator of programs promoting career awareness, training, and a positive industry image.
NPES—The Association for Suppliers of Printing, Publishing
    and Converting Technologies
1899 Preston White Drive
Reston, VA 20191-4326
Tel: 703-264-7200
E-mail: npes@npes.org
http://www.npes.org

For information on the printing industry, contact
Printing Industries of America
200 Deer Run Road
Sewickley, PA 15143-2324
Tel: 800-910-4283
E-mail: printing@printing.org
http://www.printing.org

For information on education and careers in the graphic communications industry, visit
GraphicCOMMCentral
1899 Preston White Drive
Reston, VA 20191-4326
Tel: 703-264-7200
http://www.graphiccommcentral.org

Printing Press Operators and Assistants

OVERVIEW

Printing press operators and *printing press operator assistants*, also called *printing machine operators*, prepare, operate, and maintain printing presses. Their principal duties include installing and adjusting printing plates, loading and feeding paper, mixing inks and controlling ink flow, and ensuring the quality of the final printed piece.

There are approximately 195,600 printing press operators in the United States. They are mostly employed by newspaper plants, paper manufacturing companies, and commercial and business printers.

HISTORY

The forerunners of today's modern printing presses were developed in Germany in the 15th century. They made use of the new concept of movable type, an invention generally credited to Johannes Gutenberg. Before Gutenberg's time, most books were copied by hand or printed from carved wooden blocks. Movable type used separate pieces of metal that could be easily set in place, locked into a form for printing, and then used again for another job.

The first presses consisted of two flat surfaces. Once set in place, the type was inked with a roller, and a sheet of paper was pressed against the type with a lever. Two people working together could print about 300 pages a day.

In the early 19th century, Friedrich Konig, another German, developed the first cylinder press. With a cylinder press, the paper is mounted on a large cylinder that is rolled over a flat printing surface.

The first rotary press was developed in the United States in 1865 by William Bullock. On this kind of press, the inked surface is on a revolving cylinder called a plate cylinder. The plate cylinder acts like a roller and prints onto a continuous sheet of paper (called a web) coming off a giant roll.

The speed and economy of the web press was improved by the discovery of offset printing in the early 20th century. In this process, the raised metal type used in earlier processes was substituted with a flexible plate that could be easily attached to the plate cylinder. The ink is transferred from the plate onto a rubber cylinder (called a blanket) and then onto the paper. The printing plate never touches the paper but is "offset" by the rubber blanket.

Offset printing uses the process of lithography, in which the plate is chemically treated so that ink sticks only to the parts that are to be printed and is repelled by the nonprint areas.

Offset lithography is the most common form of printing today and is used on both webfed and sheetfed presses. Webfed presses are used for newspapers and other large-volume, lower cost runs. The fastest web presses today can print about 150,000 complete newspapers in an hour. Sheetfed presses, which print on single sheets of paper rather than a continuous roll, are used for smaller, higher quality jobs.

Other forms of printing are gravure (in which depressions on an etched plate are inked and pressed to paper), flexography (a form of rotary printing using flexible rubber plates with raised image areas and fast-drying inks), screen printing (which is used to print designs on clothing, hats, and other fabric items), and letterpress (the most traditional method, in which a plate with raised, inked images is pressed against paper). Digital printing, also known as variable data printing, is the newest development in printing. In digital printing, no plates are used to print jobs. Ink is applied directly to the printing surface (such as paper). Digital printing is the fastest-growing printing specialty. It is mostly used for personal printing needs, print-on-demand jobs, and in-house corporate printing. It is considered too cost-prohibitive for large printing jobs.

THE JOB

The duties of press operators and their assistants vary according to the size of the printing plant in which they work. Generally, they are involved in all aspects of making the presses ready for a job and monitoring and operating the presses during the print run. Because

A press operator (*right*) adjusts the flow of the ink on a press as he and a manufacturing manager compare freshly printed copies of a publication with proof copies. (*Kimm Anderson,* St. Cloud Times/*AP Photo*)

most presses now are computerized, the work of press operators involves both electronic and manual processes.

In small shops, press operators usually handle all of the tasks associated with running a press, including cleaning and oiling the parts, ensuring that printing software is updated and working properly, and making minor repairs. In larger shops, press operators are aided by assistants who handle most maintenance and cleanup tasks.

Once the press has been inspected and the printing plate arrives from the platemaker, the "makeready" process begins. In this stage, the operators mount the plates into place on the printing surface or cylinder. They mix and match the ink, fill the ink fountains, and adjust the ink flow and dampening systems. They also load the paper, adjust the press to the paper size, feed the paper through the cylinders and, on a web press, adjust the tension controls. When this is done, a proof sheet is run off for the customer's review.

If a digital printing process is being used, most of the aforementioned steps required when printing with plates are automated. The operator receives the customer-approved digital file from the prepress worker and uses computer software to prepare the file for printing.

When the proof has been approved and final adjustments have been made, the press run begins. During the run, press operators constantly check the quality of the printed sheets and make any necessary adjustments. They look to see that the print is clear and properly positioned and that ink is not offsetting (blotting) onto other sheets. If the job involves color, they make sure that the colors line up properly with the images they are assigned to (registration). Operators also monitor the chemical properties of the ink and correct temperatures in the drying chamber, if the press has one.

On a web press, the feeding and tension mechanisms must be continually monitored. If the paper tears or jams, it must be rethreaded. As a roll of paper runs out, a new one must be spliced onto the old one. In large web printing plants, it takes an entire crew of specialized operators to oversee the process.

Most printing plants now have computerized printing presses equipped with sophisticated instrumentation. Press operators work at a control panel that monitors the printing processes and can adjust each variable automatically.

REQUIREMENTS

High School

The minimum educational requirement for printing press operators and assistants is a high school diploma. Students interested in this field should take courses that offer an introduction to printing and color theory, as well as chemistry, electronics, mathematics, and physics—any course that develops mechanical and mathematical aptitude. Computer science courses are especially important since many printing jobs are carefully monitored and managed using high-tech computer technology.

Postsecondary Training

Traditionally, press operators learned their craft through apprenticeship programs ranging from four to five years. Apprenticeships are still available, but they are being phased out by postsecondary programs in printing equipment operation offered by technical and trade schools and community and junior colleges. Information on apprenticeships is often available through state employment services and local chapters of printing industry associations. Additionally, many press operators and assistants still receive informal on-the-job training after a printer hires them.

Certification or Licensing

The National Council for Skill Standards in Graphic Communications has established a list of competencies—what an operator should know and be able to do—for the expert level of performance.

Skill standards are available for sheetfed and web offset press, flexographic press, and finishing and distribution. Operators can take an examination in flexographic press operation, sheet lithographic press operation, or web lithographic press operation to receive the designation of national council certified operator. The Flexographic Technical Association also provides certification.

Other Requirements

Strong communication skills, both verbal and written, are a must for press operators and assistants. They also must be able to work well as a team, both with each other and with others in the printing company. Any miscommunication during the printing process can be costly if it means rerunning a job or any part of it. Working well under pressure is another requirement because most print jobs run on tight deadlines.

EXPLORING

High school is a good time to begin exploring the occupation of printing press operator. Some schools offer print shop classes, which provide the most direct exposure to this work. Working on your high school newspaper or yearbook is another way to gain a familiarity with the printing process. A delivery job with a print shop or a visit to a local printing plant will offer you the chance to see presses in action and get a feel for the environment in which press operators work. You also might consider a part-time, temporary, or summer job as a cleanup worker or press feeder in a printing plant.

EMPLOYERS

There are approximately 195,600 press operators employed in the United States. The bulk of these work for newspaper publisher, paper manufacturing companies, and commercial and business printers. Companies range from small print shops, where one or two press operators handle everything, to large corporations that employ teams of press operators to work around the clock.

Other press operator jobs are with in-plant operations, that is, in companies and organizations that do their own printing in-house.

Because printing is so geographically diverse, press operator jobs are available in almost any city or town in the country. However, according to the *Occupational Outlook Handbook*, presswork is concentrated in large printing centers like New York, Chicago, Los Angeles, Philadelphia, Los Angeles-Long Beach, Minneapolis-St. Paul, Boston, and Washington, D.C.

STARTING OUT

Openings for trainee positions may be listed in newspaper want ads or with your state's employment service. Trade school graduates may find jobs through their school's career services office. And industry association Web sites often provide job listings.

ADVANCEMENT

Most printing press operators, even those with some training, begin their careers doing entry-level work, such as loading, unloading, and cleaning the presses. In large print shops, the line of promotion is usually as follows: press helper, press assistant, press operator, press operator-in-charge, press room supervisor, superintendent.

Press operators can advance in salary and responsibility level by learning to work more complex printing equipment, for example, by moving from a one-color press to a four-color press. Printing press operators should be prepared to continue their training and education throughout their careers. As printing companies upgrade their equipment and buy new, more computerized presses, retraining will be essential.

Press operators who are interested in other aspects of the printing business also may find advancement opportunities elsewhere in their company. Those with business savvy may be successful in establishing their own print shops.

EARNINGS

Pay rates vary for press operators, depending on their level of experience and responsibility, type of company, where they live, and whether they are union members. Median annual earnings of press operators were $32,970 in 2009, according to the U.S. Department of Labor (DOL). Salaries ranged from less than $19,840 to $53,310 or more. Printing press operators employed by newspaper, periodical, book, and directory publishers earned mean annual salaries of $38,490.

Benefits for full-time workers include vacation and sick time, health, and sometimes dental, insurance, and pension or 401(k) plans.

WORK ENVIRONMENT

Pressrooms are well ventilated, well lit, and humidity controlled. They are also noisy. Often press operators must wear ear protectors. Presswork can be physically strenuous and requires a lot of standing.

Press operators also have considerable contact with ink and cleaning fluids that can cause skin and eye irritation.

Working around large machines can be hazardous, so press operators must constantly observe good safety habits.

An eight-hour day is typical for most press operators, but some work longer hours. Smaller plants generally have only a day shift, but many larger plants and newspaper printers run around the clock. At these plants, like in hospitals and factories, press operator shifts are broken into day, afternoon/evening, and "graveyard" hours.

OUTLOOK

The DOL predicts that employment of press operators will decline moderately through 2018. An increased demand for printed materials—advertising, direct mail pieces, computer software packaging, books, and magazines—will be offset by the use of larger, more efficient machines. Additionally, new business practices such as printing-on-demand (where materials are printed in smaller amounts as they are requested by customers instead of being printed in large runs that may not be used) and electronic publishing (the publication of materials on the Internet or through other electronic methods of dissemination) will also limit opportunities for workers in this field.

Despite this prediction, there should continue to be good opportunities as many printing press operators near retirement age or leave the field for other reasons.

Newcomers to the field are likely to encounter stiff competition from experienced workers or workers who have completed retraining programs to update their skills. Opportunities are expected to be greatest for students who have completed formal apprenticeships or postsecondary training programs and who are proficient with the computer technology used in the printing process.

FOR MORE INFORMATION

This trade association represents trade binders, loose-leaf manufacturers, and suppliers throughout the United States, Canada, and Europe. For industry news and other resources, contact

Binding Industries Association
200 Deer Run Road
Sewickley, PA 15143-2324
Tel: 800-910-4283
E-mail: printing@printing.org
http://www.printing.org/node/3678

For information on flexographic printing and certification, contact
Flexographic Technical Association
900 Marconi Avenue
Ronkonkoma, NY 11779-7212
Tel: 631-737-6020
http://www.flexography.org

This union represents U.S. and Canadian workers in all craft and skill areas of the printing and publishing industries. For information on education and training programs available through local union schools, contact
Graphic Communications Conference of the International Brotherhood of Teamsters
25 Louisiana Avenue, NW
Washington, DC 20001-2130
Tel: 202-624-6800
http://www.teamster.org/content/graphics-communications

This trade association of graphic communications and graphic arts supplier companies offers economic and management information, publications, and industry reports and studies.
IPA, The Association of Graphic Solutions Providers
7200 France Avenue South, Suite 223
Edina, MN 55435-4309
Tel: 800-255-8141
http://www.ipa.org

This graphic arts trade association is a good source of general information.
National Association for Printing Leadership (NAPL)
75 West Century Road, Suite 100
Paramus, NJ 07652-1461
Tel: 800-642-6275
http://public.napl.org

This coalition serves as a clearinghouse, resource center, and coordinator of programs promoting career awareness, training, and a positive industry image.
NPES—The Association for Suppliers of Printing, Publishing and Converting Technologies
1899 Preston White Drive
Reston, VA 20191-4326
Tel: 703-264-7200

E-mail: npes@npes.org
http://www.npes.org

For information on the printing industry, contact
Printing Industries of America
200 Deer Run Road
Sewickley, PA 15143-2324
Tel: 800-910-4283
E-mail: printing@printing.org
http://www.printing.org

For information on education and careers in the graphic communi-cations industry, visit
GraphicCOMMCentral
1899 Preston White Drive
Reston, VA 20191-4326
Tel: 703-264-7200
http://www.graphiccommcentral.org

Radio and Television Program Directors

QUICK FACTS

School Subjects
Business
Journalism

Personal Skills
Communication/ideas
Leadership/management

Work Environment
Primarily indoors
Primarily one location

Minimum Education Level
Bachelor's degree

Salary Range
$12,000 to $74,190 to
$200,000

Certification or Licensing
None available

Outlook
More slowly than the average

DOT
184

GOE
01.01.01

NOC
2263

O*NET-SOC
27-2012.03

OVERVIEW

Radio and television program directors plan and schedule program material for stations and networks. They determine the news broadcasts, entertainment programs, and other program material their organizations offer to the public. At a large network, the program director may supervise a programming staff. At a small station, one person may manage the station and also handle all programming duties.

HISTORY

Radio broadcasting in the United States began after World War I. The first commercial radio station, KDKA in Pittsburgh, came on the air in 1920 with a broadcast of presidential election returns. About a dozen radio stations were broadcasting by 1921. In 1926 the first national network linked stations across the country. According to the *CIA World Factbook*, there were 4,789 AM and 8,961 FM stations broadcasting in the United States in 2006.

The first public demonstration of television in the United States came in 1939 at the opening of the New York World's Fair. Further development was limited during World War II, but by 1953 there were about 120 stations. According to the *CIA World Factbook*, there were 2,218 television broadcast stations in the United States in 2006. The National Cable and Telecommunications Association reports that between 2002 and 2007, the number of cable networks nearly doubled, from 287 to 565 channels.

Top Radio Markets, Spring 2010

1. New York, N.Y.
2. Los Angeles, Calif.
3. Chicago, Ill.
4. San Francisco, Calif.
5. Dallas-Ft. Worth, Tex.
6. Houston-Galveston, Tex.
7. Atlanta, Ga.
8. Philadelphia, Pa.
9. Washington, D.C.
10. Boston, Mass.

Source: Arbitron (by population)

THE JOB

Program directors plan and schedule program material for radio and television stations and networks. They work in both commercial and public broadcasting and may be employed by individual radio or television stations, regional or national networks, or cable television systems.

The material program directors work with includes newscasts, sportscasts, entertainment programs, public service programs, and commercial announcements. Program directors decide what material is broadcast and when it is scheduled; they work with other staff members to develop programs and buy programs from independent producers. They are guided by such factors as the budget available for program material, the audience their station or network seeks to attract, their organization's policies on content and other matters, and the kinds of products advertised in the various commercial announcements.

In addition, program directors may set up schedules for the program staff, audition and hire announcers and other on-the-air personnel, and assist the sales department in negotiating contracts with sponsors of commercial announcements. The duties of individual program directors are determined by such factors as whether they work in radio or television, for a small or large organization, for one station or a network, or in a commercial or public operation.

At small radio stations the owner or manager may be responsible for programming, but at larger radio stations and at television stations the staff usually includes a program director. At medium to large radio and television stations the program director usually has a staff that includes such personnel as music librarians, music directors, editors for recorded segments, and writers. Some stations and networks employ public service directors. It is the responsibility of these individuals to plan and schedule radio or television public service programs and announcements in such fields as education, religion, and civic and government affairs. Networks often employ *broadcast operations directors*, who coordinate the activities of the personnel who prepare network program schedules, review program schedules, issue daily corrections, and advise affiliated stations on their schedules.

Program directors must carefully coordinate the various elements for a station while keeping in tune with the listeners, viewers, advertisers, and sponsors.

In journalistic settings, program directors work closely with *news directors*. These workers oversee news teams (reporters, producers, photographers, editors, writers, newscasters, and announcers) at radio and television stations. They are responsible for the look/sound and content of the broadcast, as well as overseeing its technical elements. Directors need a sense of dramatics, combined with the ability to weld together into a smooth and artistic production

Top Television Markets, 2010

1. New York, N.Y.
2. Los Angeles, Calif.
3. Chicago, Ill.
4. Philadelphia, Pa.
5. Dallas-Ft. Worth, Tex.
6. San Francisco-Oakland-San Jose, Calif.
7. Boston, Mass.
8. Atlanta, Ga.
9. Washington, D.C.
10. Houston, Tex.

Source: Nielsen Media Research (by population)

the creative talents of performers and behind-the-scenes personnel under deadline pressure.

Other managers in radio and television broadcasting include *production managers, operations directors*, and *sports directors*.

REQUIREMENTS

High School

If you are interested in this career, you should take courses that develop your communication skills in high school. Such classes include English, debate, and speech. You also should take business courses to develop your management skills; current events and history courses to develop your understanding of the news and the trends that affect the public's interests; and such courses as dance, drama, music, and painting to expand your understanding of the creative arts. Finally, do not neglect your computer skills. You will probably be using computers throughout your career to file reports, maintain schedules, and plan future programming projects.

Postsecondary Training

Those with the most thorough educational backgrounds will find it easiest to advance in this field. A college degree, therefore, is recommended for this field. Possible majors for those interested in this work include radio and television production and broadcasting, communications, journalism, liberal arts, or business administration. You will probably take English, economics, business administration, computer, and media classes. You may also wish to acquire some technical training that will help you understand the engineering aspects of broadcasting.

Other Requirements

Program directors must be creative, alert, and adaptable people who stay up-to-date on the public's interests and attitudes and are able to recognize the potential in new ideas. They must be able to work under pressure and be willing to work long hours with all kinds of people. Program directors also must be good managers who can make decisions, oversee costs and deadlines, and attend to details.

EXPLORING

If your high school or college has a radio or television station, you should volunteer to work on the staff. You also should look for part-time or summer jobs at local radio or television stations. You may not be able to plan the programming at a local station, but you will see how a station works and be able to make contacts with those in the field. If you cannot find a job at a local station, at least arrange for a visit and ask to talk to the personnel. You may be able to "shadow" a program director for a day—that is, follow that director for the workday and see what his or her job entails.

EMPLOYERS

According to the *CIA World Factbook*, there were 2,218 broadcast television stations and 13,750 radio stations in the United States in 2006. Cable television stations provide another option for employment.

Large conglomerates own some stations, while others are owned individually. Although radio and television stations are located all over the country, the largest stations with the highest paid positions are located in large metropolitan areas.

STARTING OUT

Program director jobs are not entry-level positions. A degree and extensive experience in the field is required. Most program directors have technical and on-air experience in either radio or television. While you are in college you should investigate the availability of internships, since internships are almost essential for prospective job candidates. Your college's career services office should also have information on job openings. Private and state employment agencies may also prove useful resources. You can also send your resume to radio and television stations or apply in person.

Beginners should be willing to relocate, as they are unlikely to find employment in large cities. They usually start at small stations with fewer employees, allowing them a chance to learn a variety of skills.

Additionally, the Radio Television Digital News Association offers job listings at its Web site, http://www.rtdna.org.

ADVANCEMENT

Most beginners start in entry-level jobs and work several years before they have enough experience to become program directors. Experienced program directors usually advance by moving from small stations to larger stations and networks or by becoming station managers.

EARNINGS

Salaries for radio and television program directors vary widely based on such factors as size and location of the station, whether the station is commercial or public, and experience of the director. Television program directors generally earn more than their counterparts in radio. According to the U.S. Department of Labor (DOL), mean annual earnings of program directors in radio and television broadcasting were $74,190 in 2009. All producers and directors earned salaries that ranged from less than $30,560 to $166,400 or more.

According to a salary survey by Radio Television Digital News Association and Hofstra University, radio news directors earned a median salary of $31,000, and salaries ranged from a low of $19,000 to a high of $95,000 in 2009. Television news directors earned a median of $76,000, with salaries ranging from $12,000 to $200,000.

Both radio and television program directors usually receive health and life insurance benefits and sometimes yearly bonuses as well.

WORK ENVIRONMENT

Program directors at small stations often work 44 to 48 hours a week and frequently work evenings, late at night, and weekends. At larger stations, which have more personnel, program directors usually work 40-hour weeks.

Program directors frequently work under pressure because of the need to maintain precise timing and meet the needs of sponsors, performers, and other staff members.

Although the work is sometimes stressful and demanding, program directors usually work in pleasant environments with creative staffs. They also interact with the community to arrange programming and deal with a variety of people.

OUTLOOK

All radio and television stations, cable television systems, and regional and national networks employ program directors or have other employees whose duties include programming. According to the DOL, employment in broadcasting is expected to increase 7 percent over the 2008–18 period, slower than the average of 14 percent growth for all industries combined. This slow growth rate is attributed to industry consolidation, introduction of new technologies, greater use of prepared programming, and competition from other media.

Competition for radio and television program director jobs is strong. There are more opportunities for beginners in radio than there are in television. Most radio and television stations in large cities hire only experienced workers.

New radio and television stations and new cable television systems are expected to create additional openings for program directors, but some radio stations are eliminating program director positions by installing automatic programming equipment or combining those responsibilities with other positions.

FOR MORE INFORMATION

Contact the alliance for information on careers in radio and television, as well as scholarships and internships for college students.

Alliance for Women in Media (formerly American Women in Radio and Television)
1760 Old Meadow Road, Suite 500
McLean, VA 22102-4306
Tel: 703-506-3290
http://www.awrt.org

An association of university broadcasting faculty, industry professionals, and graduate students, BEA offers annual scholarships in broadcasting for college juniors, seniors, and graduate students. Visit its Web site for useful information about broadcast education and the broadcasting industry.

Broadcast Education Association (BEA)
1771 N Street, NW
Washington, DC 20036-2891
Tel: 202-429-3935
http://www.beaweb.org

The association provides information on broadcast education, scholarships for college students, jobs, and useful publications at its Web site.

National Association of Broadcasters
1771 N Street, NW
Washington, DC 20036-2800
Tel: 202-429-5300
E-mail: nab@nab.org
http://www.nab.org

Contact the association for information on farm broadcasting and membership, scholarships, and internships for college students.

National Association of Farm Broadcasting
700 Branch Street, Suite 8
PO Box 500
Platte City, MO 64079-0500
Tel: 816-431-4032
E-mail: info@nafb.com
http://nafb.com

Visit the NCTA Web site for information on careers in the cable industry.

National Cable and Telecommunications Association (NCTA)
25 Massachusetts Avenue, NW, Suite 100
Washington, DC 20001-1434
Tel: 202-222-2300
http://www.ncta.com

Visit this organization's Web site to access scholarship and internship information (for college students), high school journalism resources and programs (such as the High School Broadcast Journalism Project), useful publications, and salary and employment surveys. The association also offers membership to college students.

Radio Television Digital News Association
529 14th Street, NW, Suite 425
Washington, DC 20045-1406
Tel: 202-659-6510
http://www.rtdna.org

Reporters

QUICK FACTS

School Subjects
English
Journalism

Personal Skills
Communication/ideas
Helping/teaching

Work Environment
Indoors and outdoors
Primarily multiple locations

Minimum Education Level
Bachelor's degree

Salary Range
$19,650 to $34,360 to
$74,700+

Certification or Licensing
None available

Outlook
Decline

DOT
131

GOE
01.03.01

NOC
5123

O*NET-SOC
27-3020.00, 27-3021.00,
27-3022.00

OVERVIEW

Reporters, who are also called *journalists* and *correspondents*, are the foot soldiers for newspapers, magazines, television and radio broadcast companies, and journalism Web sites. They gather and analyze information about current events and write stories for publication or for broadcasting. Reporters and correspondents hold approximately 61,600 jobs in the United States.

HISTORY

Newspapers are some of the primary disseminators of news in the United States. People read newspapers to learn about the current events that are shaping their society and societies around the world. Newspapers give public expression to opinion and criticism of government and societal issues, and, of course, provide the public with entertaining, informative reading.

Newspapers are able to fulfill these functions because of the freedom given to the press. However, this was not always the case. The first American newspaper, published in 1690, was suppressed four days after it was published. And it was not until 1704 that the first continuous newspaper appeared.

One early newspaperman who later became a famous writer was Benjamin Franklin. Franklin worked for his brother at a Boston newspaper before publishing his own paper two years later in 1723 in Philadelphia.

A number of developments in the printing industry made it possible for newspapers to be printed more cheaply. In the late 19th century, new types of presses were developed to increase production, and more importantly, the Linotype machine was invented. The

Linotype mechanically set letters so that handset type was no longer necessary. This dramatically decreased the amount of prepress time needed to get a page into print. Newspapers could respond to breaking stories more quickly, and late editions with breaking stories became part of the news world.

These technological advances, along with an increasing population, factored into the rapid growth of the newspaper industry in the United States. In 1776, there were only 37 newspapers in the United States. Today there are more than 1,422 daily newspapers in the country.

As newspapers grew in size and widened the scope of their coverage, it became necessary to increase the number of employees and to assign them specialized jobs. Reporters have always been the heart of newspaper staffs. However, in today's complex world, with the public hungry for news as it occurs, reporters and correspondents are involved in all media—not only newspapers, but also magazines, radio, and television as well. Today, most newspapers are available online, creating many opportunities for reporting on the Web.

THE JOB

Reporters collect information on newsworthy events and prepare stories for newspaper or magazine publication or for radio or television broadcast. The stories may simply provide information about local, state, or national events, or they may present opposing points of view on issues of current interest. In this latter capacity, the press plays an important role in monitoring the actions of public officials and others in positions of power.

Stories may originate as an assignment from an editor or as the result of a lead or news tip. Good reporters are always on the lookout for good story ideas. To cover a story, they gather and verify facts by interviewing people involved in or related to the event, examining documents and public records, observing events as they happen, and researching relevant background information. Reporters generally take notes or use a recorder as they collect information and write their stories once they return to their offices. After the facts have been gathered and verified, the reporters transcribe their notes, organize their material, and determine what emphasis, or angle, to give the news. The story is then written to meet prescribed standards of editorial style and format.

The basic functions of reporters are to observe events objectively and impartially, record them accurately, and explain what the news means in a larger, societal context. Within this framework, there are several types of reporters.

The most basic is the *news reporter*. This job sometimes involves covering a beat, which means that the reporter may be assigned to consistently cover news from an area such as the local courthouse, police station, or school system. It may involve receiving general assignments, such as a story about an unusual occurrence or an obituary of a community leader. Large daily papers and television stations may assign teams of reporters to investigate social, economic, or political events and conditions.

Many newspaper, wire service, and magazine reporters specialize in one type of story, either because they have a particular interest in the subject or because they have acquired the expertise to analyze and interpret news in that particular area. *Topical reporters* cover stories for a specific department, such as medicine, politics, foreign affairs, sports, consumer affairs, finance, science, business, education, labor, or religion. They sometimes write features explaining the history that has led up to certain events in the field they cover. *Feature writers* generally write longer, broader stories than news reporters, usually on more upbeat subjects, such as fashion, art, theater, travel, and social events. They may write about trends, for example, or profile local celebrities. *Editorial writers* and *syndicated news columnists* present viewpoints that, although based on a thorough knowledge, are opinions on topics of popular interest. *Columnists* write under a byline and usually specialize in a particular subject such as politics or government activities. *Critics* review restaurants, books, works of art, movies, plays, musical performances, and other cultural events.

In radio and television, reporters may specialize in covering business, health, sports, weather, entertainment, politics, or other fields.

Specializing allows reporters to focus their efforts, talent, and knowledge on one area of expertise. It also gives them more opportunities to develop deeper relationships with contacts and sources, which is necessary to gain access to the news.

Correspondents report events in locations distant from their home offices. They may report news by mail, telephone, fax, or computer from rural areas, large cities throughout the United States, or countries. Many large newspapers, magazines, and broadcast companies have one correspondent who is responsible for covering all the news for the foreign city or country where they are based. These reporters are known as *foreign correspondents*.

Reporters on small or weekly newspapers not only cover all aspects of the news in their communities, but also may take photographs and video, write editorials and headlines, lay out pages, edit wire-service copy, and help with general office work. *Television reporters* may have to be photogenic as well as talented and resourceful; they may at times present live reports, filmed by a mobile camera unit at the scene where the news originates, or they may record interviews and narration for later broadcast.

REQUIREMENTS

High School

High school courses that will provide you with a firm foundation for a reporting career include English, journalism, history, computer science, social studies, communications, political science, geography, typing, and computer science. Speech courses will help you hone your interviewing skills, which are necessary for success as a reporter, as well as to effectively communicate with audiences if you work in broadcast journalism. In addition, it will be helpful to take college preparatory courses, such as foreign language, math, and science.

Postsecondary Training

You will need at least a bachelor's degree to become a reporter, and a graduate degree will give you a great advantage over those entering the field with lesser degrees. Most editors prefer applicants with degrees in journalism because their studies include liberal arts courses as well as professional training in journalism. Some editors consider it sufficient for a reporter to have a good general education from a liberal arts college. Others prefer applicants with an undergraduate degree in liberal arts and a master's degree in journalism. The great majority of journalism graduates hired today by newspapers, wire services, and magazines have majored specifically in news-editorial journalism.

More than 1,500 colleges offer programs in journalism, communications, or related fields. In these schools, around three-fourths of a student's time is devoted to a liberal arts education and one-fourth to the professional study of journalism, with required courses such as introductory mass media, basic reporting and copyediting, history of journalism, and press law and ethics. Students are encouraged to select other journalism courses according to their specific interests. Visit the Web site of the Accrediting Council on Education in Journalism and Mass Communications (http://www2.ku.edu/~acejmc/STUDENT/PROGLIST.SHTML) for a list of accredited postsecondary training programs in journalism and mass communications.

Approximately 200 colleges offer programs in broadcast journalism leading to a bachelor's degree. Broadcast programs require

A reporter conducts an interview at a political rally. *(Bob Daemmrich, The Image Works)*

students to take courses like reporting, photography, ethics, and broadcast history. Many schools also have TV and radio stations that either employ students or offer students credit for their work.

Journalism courses and programs are also offered by many community and junior colleges. Graduates of these programs are prepared to go to work directly as general assignment reporters, but they may encounter difficulty when competing with graduates of four-year programs. Credit earned in community and junior colleges may be transferable to four-year programs in journalism at other colleges and universities. Journalism training may also be obtained in the armed forces. Names and addresses of newspapers and a list of journalism schools and departments are published in the annual *Editor & Publisher International Year Book: The Encyclopedia of the Newspaper Industry* (New York: Editor & Publisher), which is available for reference in most public libraries and newspaper offices.

Master's degree and Ph.D. programs are also available. Graduate degrees may prepare students specifically for careers in news or as journalism teachers, researchers, and theorists, or for jobs in advertising or public relations.

A reporter's liberal arts training should include courses in English (with an emphasis on writing), sociology, political science, economics, history, psychology, business, speech, and computer science. Knowledge of foreign languages is also useful. To be a reporter in a specialized field, such as science or finance, requires concentrated course work in that area.

Other Requirements

In order to succeed as a reporter, it is crucial that you have good typing skills, as you will type your stories using word processing programs. Although not essential, a knowledge of shorthand or speedwriting makes note taking easier, and an acquaintance with news photography and videography is an asset.

Reporters are levelheaded and able to keep calm in stressful situations. Broadcast reporters going live must be able to think on their feet. Reporters must also have a good understanding of topical issues, history, geography, and government. And reporters must write and speak well.

You must also be inquisitive, aggressive, persistent, and detail oriented. You should enjoy interaction with people of various races, cultures, religions, economic levels, and social statuses.

EXPLORING

You can explore a career as a reporter in a number of ways. You can talk to reporters and editors at local newspapers and radio and TV stations. You can interview the admissions counselor at the school of journalism closest to your home.

In addition to taking courses in English, journalism, social studies, speech, computer science, and typing, high school students can acquire practical experience by working on school newspapers or on a church, synagogue, or mosque newsletter. Part-time and summer jobs on newspapers provide invaluable experience to the aspiring reporter.

Working for your radio station will provide you with valuable experience interviewing, editing, and writing. Also, become familiar with video and recording equipment by working for your high school's media department.

College students can develop their reporting skills in the laboratory courses or workshops that are part of the journalism curriculum. College students might also accept jobs as campus correspondents for selected newspapers or college radio or television stations. People who work as part-time reporters covering news in a particular area of a community are known as *stringers* and are paid only for those stories that are printed.

Thousands of scholarships, fellowships, and assistantships are offered by universities, newspapers, foundations, and professional organizations to college students. Many newspapers and magazines offer summer internships to journalism students to provide them with practical experience in a variety of basic reporting and editing duties. Students who successfully complete internships are usually placed in jobs more quickly upon graduation than those without such experience.

EMPLOYERS

Of the approximately 61,600 reporters and correspondents employed in the United States, about 53 percent work for newspaper, periodical, book, and directory publishers. Approximately 21 percent work in radio and television broadcasting. The rest are employed by wire services.

STARTING OUT

Jobs in this field may be obtained through college career services offices or by applying directly to the personnel departments of individual employers. If you have some practical experience, you will have an advantage; you should be prepared to present a portfolio of material you wrote as a volunteer or part-time reporter, or other writing or broadcasting samples.

Most journalism school graduates start out as general assignment reporters for print and broadcasting employers or copy editors for small publications. A few outstanding journalism graduates may be hired by large city newspapers, national magazines, or broadcasting companies in large media markets. They are trained on the job. But they are the exception, as large employers usually require several years' experience. As a rule, novice reporters cover routine assignments, such as reporting on civic and club meetings, writing obituaries, or summarizing speeches. As you become more skilled in reporting, you will be assigned to more important events or to a regular beat, or you may specialize in a particular field.

ADVANCEMENT

Newspaper and magazine reporters may advance by moving to larger newspapers or press services, but competition for such positions is unusually keen. Many highly qualified reporters apply for these jobs every year.

A select number of reporters eventually become columnists, correspondents, editorial writers, editors, or top executives. These important and influential positions represent the top of the field, and competition is strong for them.

Within a local TV or radio station, a reporter may eventually move on to another area of broadcasting, such as directing or producing a newscast. Reporters also become anchors, who are better paid and more prominent in the newscast. Many more people are employed in sales, promotion, and planning than are employed in reporting and anchoring; and people in sales and management positions often draw a better salary than the journalists.

Many reporters transfer the contacts and knowledge developed in reporting to related fields, such as public relations or advertising.

EARNINGS

There are great variations in the earnings of reporters. Salaries are related to experience, the type of employer for which the reporter works, geographic location, and whether the reporter is covered by a contract negotiated by The Newspaper Guild or other unions.

According to the U.S. Department of Labor, the median salary for reporters and correspondents was $34,360 in 2009. The lowest paid 10 percent of these workers earned $19,650 or less per year, while the highest paid 10 percent made $74,700 or more annually. Reporters and correspondents employed in radio and television had mean annual earnings of $51,570 in 2009. Those employed by newspaper, periodical, book, and directory publishers earned $39,120 a year.

Benefits for full-time workers include vacation and sick time, health, and sometimes dental, insurance, and pension or 401(k) plans. Self-employed reporters must provide their own benefits.

WORK ENVIRONMENT

Reporters work under a great deal of pressure in settings that differ from the typical business office. Their jobs generally require a five-day, 35- to 40-hour week, but overtime and irregular schedules are very common. Reporters employed by morning papers start work in the late afternoon and finish around midnight, while those on afternoon or evening papers start early in the morning and work until early or mid-afternoon. Broadcast journalists work a variety of shifts, ranging from early morning, to midday, to the evening. Foreign correspondents often work late at night to send the news to their papers or broadcast outlets in time to meet printing or broadcast deadlines.

Reporters have to work amid the clatter of computer keyboards and other machines, loud voices engaged in telephone conversations, and the bustle created by people hurrying about. An atmosphere of excitement prevails, especially as press or broadcast deadlines approach.

Travel is often required in this occupation, and assignments such as covering wars, political uprisings, fires, floods, and other events of a volatile nature may be dangerous.

OUTLOOK

Employment for reporters and correspondents through 2018 is expected to decline, according to the *Occupational Outlook Handbook*. While the number of self-employed reporters and correspondents is expected to grow, newspaper jobs are expected to decrease because of mergers, consolidations, and closures in the newspaper and magazine industries.

Because of an increase in the number of small community and suburban daily and weekly newspapers, opportunities will be best for journalism graduates who are willing to relocate and accept relatively low starting salaries. With experience, reporters on these small papers can move up to editing positions or may choose to transfer to reporting jobs on larger newspapers or magazines.

Openings will be limited on big city dailies. While individual papers may enlarge their reporting staffs, little or no change is expected in the total number of these newspapers. Applicants will face strong competition for jobs on large metropolitan newspapers. Experience is a definite requirement, which rules out most new graduates unless they possess credentials in an area for which the publication has a pressing need. Occasionally, a beginner can use contacts and experience gained through internship programs and summer jobs to obtain a reporting job immediately after graduation.

Employment is expected to be only fair in radio and television broadcasting. Industry consolidation and declining ad revenues are forcing stations to do more with less, which is reducing the number of reporters in the industry. For beginning correspondents, small stations with local news broadcasts will continue to replace staff who move on to larger stations or leave the business. Network hiring has been cut drastically in the past few years and will probably continue to decline. Stronger employment growth is expected for reporters in online newspapers and magazines.

Overall, the prospects are best for graduates who have majored in news-editorial journalism and completed an internship while in school. The top graduates in an accredited program will have a great advantage, as will talented technical and scientific writers. Small newspapers prefer to hire beginning reporters who are acquainted with the community and are willing to help with photography and other aspects of production. Without at least a bachelor's degree in journalism, applicants will find it increasingly difficult to obtain even an entry-level position.

Technology will continue to have a big impact on the way news is reported. The development of satellite technology and portable high-definition video cameras has revolutionized broadcast journalism over the last 30 years, and new developments over the next 20 years will likely have the same powerful effects. As the Internet competes for TV's viewers and radio's listeners, look for newsrooms to make better use of the technology. Aspiring reporters should learn how to work with audio and video recording technology and digital cameras, and be able to conduct research on the Internet.

Those with doctorates and practical reporting experience may find teaching positions at four-year colleges and universities, while highly qualified reporters with master's degrees may obtain employment in journalism departments of community and junior colleges.

FOR MORE INFORMATION

For a list of accredited programs in journalism and mass communications, visit the ACEJMC Web site.
Accrediting Council on Education in Journalism and
    Mass Communications (ACEJMC)
University of Kansas School of Journalism and
Mass Communications
Stauffer-Flint Hall, 1435 Jayhawk Boulevard
Lawrence, KS 66045-7575
Tel: 785-864-3973
http://www2.ku.edu/~acejmc/STUDENT/PROGLIST.SHTML

Contact the alliance for information on careers in radio and television, as well as scholarships and internships for college students.
Alliance for Women in Media (formerly American Women in
    Radio and Television)
1760 Old Meadow Road, Suite 500
McLean, VA 22102-4306
Tel: 703-506-3290
http://www.awrt.org

For information on union membership, contact
American Federation of Radio and Television Artists
260 Madison Avenue
New York NY 10016-2401
Tel: 212-532-0800
http://www.aftra.org

The society provides information on careers in reporting, as well as details on education and financial aid (from outside sources).

American Society of Journalists and Authors
1501 Broadway, Suite 302
New York, NY 10036-5505
Tel: 212-997-0947
http://www.asja.org

This organization provides general educational information on all areas of journalism, including newspapers, magazines, television, Internet, and radio. Members include journalism and mass communication faculty, administrators, students, and media professionals.

Association for Education in Journalism and
    Mass Communication
234 Outlet Pointe Boulevard, Suite A
Columbia, SC 29210-5667
Tel: 803-798-0271
E-mail: aejmchq@aol.com
http://www.aejmc.com

An association of university broadcasting faculty, industry professionals, and graduate students, BEA offers annual scholarships in broadcasting for college juniors, seniors, and graduate students. Visit its Web site for useful information about broadcast education and the broadcasting industry.

Broadcast Education Association (BEA)
1771 N Street, NW
Washington, DC 20036-2891
Tel: 202-429-3935
http://www.beaweb.org

Visit the fund's Web site for information on print and online journalism careers, college and university journalism programs, high school journalism workshops, scholarships, internships, and job listings.

Dow Jones News Fund
PO Box 300
Princeton, NJ 08543-0300
Tel: 609-452-2820
E-mail: djnf@dowjones.com
https://www.newsfund.org

Visit this organization's Web site for information on investigative journalism and scholarships and membership for college students.
Investigative Reporters and Editors
Missouri School of Journalism
141 Neff Annex
Columbia, MO 65211-0001
Tel: 573-882-2042
E-mail: info@ire.org
http://www.ire.org

Contact the association for information on union membership.
National Association of Broadcast Employees and Technicians
501 Third Street, NW
Washington, DC 20001-2760
http://nabetcwa.org

The association provides information on broadcast education, scholarships for college students, jobs, and useful publications at its Web site.
National Association of Broadcasters
1771 N Street, NW
Washington, DC 20036-2800
Tel: 202-429-5300
E-mail: nab@nab.org
http://www.nab.org

This nonprofit organization represents the $47 billion newspaper industry and more than 2,000 newspapers in the United States and Canada. Visit its Web site for information on trends in the industry and careers (including digital media job descriptions).
Newspaper Association of America
4401 Wilson Boulevard, Suite 900
Arlington, VA 22203-1867
Tel: 571-366-1000
http://www.naa.org

The guild is a union for journalists, advertising sales workers, and other media professionals.
The Newspaper Guild-Communications Workers of America
501 Third Street, NW, 6th Floor
Washington, DC 20001-2797
Tel: 202-434-7177
E-mail: guild@cwa-union.org
http://www.newsguild.org

The Online News Association is a membership organization for journalists "whose principal livelihood involves gathering or producing news for digital presentation." Members include "news writers, producers, designers, editors, photographers, technologists and others who produce news for the Internet or other digital delivery systems, as well as academic members and others interested in the development of online news." Visit its Web site for information on membership for high school and college students.

Online News Association
http://journalists.org

Visit this organization's Web site to access scholarship and internship information (for college students), high school journalism resources and programs (such as the High School Broadcast Journalism Project), useful publications, and salary and employment surveys. The association also offers membership to college students.

Radio Television Digital News Association
529 14th Street, NW, Suite 425
Washington, DC 20045-1406
Tel: 202-659-6510
http://www.rtdna.org

Visit the society's Web site for information on student chapters and scholarships for college students, job listings, training opportunities, educational resources, discussion boards and blogs, and much more.

Society of Professional Journalists
3909 North Meridian Street
Indianapolis, IN 46208-4011
Tel: 317-927-8000
http://www.spj.org

Visit the following Web site for comprehensive information on journalism careers, summer programs, and college journalism programs:

High School Journalism
http://www.hsj.org

For comprehensive information for citizens, students, and news people about the field of journalism, visit

Project for Excellence in Journalism
1615 L Street, NW, Suite 700
Washington, DC 20036-5621
Tel: 202-419-3650
E-mail: mail@journalism.org
http://www.journalism.org

INTERVIEW

Benny Evangelista is reporter at the San Francisco Chronicle. *He discussed his career with the editors of* Careers in Focus: Journalism.

Q. How long have you worked in the field? What made you want to become a journalist?

A. I've been a journalist since 1980. I always enjoyed writing, but I never thought about making a career out of it until I took a beginning journalism class in college. I immediately enjoyed the class and about midway through the semester, my professor told me I had potential and encouraged me to change my major to journalism. So I did, but I also began to realize that as a Filipino American entering a field when there were few journalists of color, I had the opportunity to help make a difference in the way mainstream media covered communities of color. So that became a mission of mine.

Q. Can you describe a typical day on the job?

A. I usually check my e-mail on my way into the office using my iPhone. I also read several Web sites that are pertinent to my current beat, do social networking, and check in with my editor to see if he's got an assignment for me or go over what I am planning to cover. From there, nothing's too typical. If I come up with a story or am assigned one, I work on it. Otherwise, I'll do some reporting on upcoming stories or beat the bushes to come up with future story ideas. Our primary task is to write stories for the newspaper, but for breaking news, we are also asked to post it as soon as possible on our Web site, SFGate.com.

Q. What are the most important personal and professional skills for reporters?

A. You must have a curiosity about the world, an insatiable appetite to keep learning all you can. You must have the tenacity to get even the toughest stories, the unbending desire to get the story right, and the compassion to know what your story will mean for the people who matter most—the readers.

Q. What is one of the most interesting or rewarding things that has happened to you while working in the field?

A. This job has given me a front row seat for modern history. I get to ask questions of top CEOs, politicians, and just regular folk.

Q. **What is the employment outlook for journalism, especially online journalism?**

A. The outlook is uncertain. For newspapers, the immediate outlook is grim, but who knows what it will be in a few years. I think the outlook for online is much better, but also uncertain, at least until we find a business model that can support the level of journalism we've been accustomed to.

Sportswriters

OVERVIEW

Sportswriters cover the news in sports for newspapers and magazines. They research original ideas or follow up on breaking stories, contacting coaches, athletes, and team owners and managers for comments or more information. Sometimes a sportswriter is fortunate enough to get his or her own column, in which the sportswriter editorializes on current news or developments in sports.

HISTORY

Throughout the world there are some 7,200 daily newspapers and far more semiweeklies, biweeklies, and weeklies, circulating at least 500 million copies on a regular basis. In the international context, the average newspaper is crude, poorly printed, heavy with sensational news, light on serious criticism, and burdened by all types of problems (especially economic). Outside Western Europe and North America there are very few "elite," or ultra serious, newspapers. Although most of the world's newspapers are privately owned, some degree of government control is evident in many countries.

Magazine journalism has been a potent force in the United States (and throughout the world), appealing mainly to the elite, the well educated, and the opinion leaders. At least this is true in the sense of "journalistic" magazines. Generally more incisive, more articulate, more interpretive, and certainly more comprehensive than newspapers, magazines have supplied an important intellectual dimension to news-oriented journalism. Whereas the main function of newspaper journalism is to inform or summarize in brief fashion, the aim of most magazine journalism is to fill gaps—to explain,

QUICK FACTS

School Subjects
English
Journalism
Physical education

Personal Skills
Communication/ideas

Work Environment
Indoors and outdoors
Primarily multiple locations

Minimum Education Level
Bachelor's degree

Salary Range
$28,070 to $53,900 to $105,710+

Certification or Licensing
None available

Outlook
About as fast as the average

DOT
131

GOE
01.03.01

NOC
5231

O*NET-SOC
27-3022.00, 27-3043.00

The Top Ten U.S. Dailies by Circulation

1. *Wall Street Journal*: 2,092,523
2. *USA Today*: 1,826,622
3. *New York Times*: 951,063
4. *Los Angeles Times*: 616,606
5. *Washington Post*: 578,482
6. *Daily News* (New York): 535,059
7. *New York Post*: 525,004
8. *San Jose Mercury News/Contra Costa Times/Oakland Tribune*: 516,701
9. *Chicago Tribune*: 516,032
10. *Houston Chronicle*: 494,131

Source: Audit Bureau of Circulation, March 2010

interpret, criticize, and comment. In short, magazine journalism in its many types and styles supplements newspapers and fleshes out the bare bones of newspaper journalism.

Most magazines and newspapers have sections that focus on sports; others, such as *Sports Illustrated* and *ESPN The Magazine*, focus entirely on sports reporting. In either case, sportswriters are needed to write articles about athletes, teams, and sports competitions. Sportswriters are employed by both newspapers and magazines throughout the United States.

THE JOB

The sportswriter's primary job is to report the outcomes of the sports events that occurred that day. Since one newspaper cannot employ enough reporters to cover, in person, every single high school, college, and professional sports event that happens on any given day, let alone sports events happening in other cities and countries, sportswriters use the newswire services to get the details. Major national and international wire services include Reuters, Associated Press, United Press International, Agence France-Presse, and ITAR-TASS. The entire body of statistics for tennis matches, hockey games, and track-and-field events, for example, can be sent over the wire service so that sportswriters can include the general story and the vital statistics in as condensed or lengthy a form as space allows.

A sportswriter begins work each day by reviewing the local, national, and international news that comes in over the newswire services. He or she then begins researching the top or lead stories to try to flesh out the story, perhaps with a local perspective on it, or to come up with a new angle or spin altogether. An example of a lead story might be the comeback of a professional tennis star; the underdog victory of a third-rate, much-maligned football team; the incredible pitching record of a high school athlete; or the details about a football running back who blew out his knee in a crucial last-minute play. The sportswriter then calls or interviews in person coaches, athletes, scouts, agents, promoters, and sometimes, in the case of an athletic injury, a physician or team of physicians.

Depending on the edition of the newspaper or magazine, the sportswriter might report events that happened anywhere from the day before to events that took place within that week or month. For example, a sportswriter who writes for a magazine such as *Sports Illustrated* probably will not write articles with the same degree of detail per game. Instead, he or she writes articles, commonly called *features*, that explore an entire season for a team or an athlete. The magazine sportswriter might take the same story of the running back with the damaged knee ligaments and follow that athlete through his surgery and rehabilitation, interviewing not only the running back, but also his wife, doctors, coaches, and agent. This stage of gathering information is the same for both newspaper and magazine sportswriters, the only difference is the time line; a newspaper sportswriter may have only a few hours to conduct research and call around for comments, while the sportswriter for a magazine may have anywhere from several weeks to several months to compose the story.

Regardless of whether the sportswriter works for a newspaper or magazine, the next step for the sportswriter is to write the story. The method will vary, again, depending on the medium. Most sportswriters for newspapers are subject to the constraints of space, and these limits can change in a matter of minutes. On a dull day, up until the hour before the paper is published (or put to bed), the sportswriter might have a quarter of a page to fill with local sports news. At the last minute, however, an entire Super Bowl team could come down with food poisoning, in which case the sports editor would probably want to cover this larger, breaking story. To accommodate the new articles about the poisoning, the effect on team morale, whether the Super Bowl might be postponed for the first time in history, the local sports coverage would either have to shrink considerably or be completely cut. (Of course, if a newspaper or magazine has a Web site, then the article can be as long as necessary.) To manage this, sportswriters, like other reporters who write for daily newspapers, compose their stories with the most crucial facts contained within the first one or two paragraphs of the story. They may write a 10-paragraph story, but if it had to be shortened, the pertinent information would be easily retained.

Sportswriters for magazines, on the other hand, seldom need to worry about their stories being cut down at the last minute. Rather, their stories are subject to more careful editing. Magazines usually have story meetings weeks or months in advance of the relevant issue, giving sportswriters ample time to plan, research, and write their articles. As a result of the different timetable, the presentation of the story will change. The sportswriter will not cram all the essential facts into an opening paragraph or two. Instead, he or she is allowed much greater leeway with the introduction and the rest of the article. The sportswriter, in this case, will want to set a mood in the introduction, developing the characters of the individuals being interviewed—literally, telling a story about the story. In short, details can hinder a newspaper sports story from accomplishing its goal of getting across the facts in a concise form, while in a magazine sports article, those extraneous, revealing details actually become part of the story.

Even with the help of news services, sportswriters still could not have all the sports news at their fingertips without the help of other reporters and writers, known in the world of reporting as *stringers*. A stringer covers an event that, most likely, would not be covered by the wire services, such as high school sports events, as well as games in professional sports that are occurring simultaneously with other major sports events. The stringer attends the sports event and phones in scores, or e-mails or faxes in a complete report.

While the sportswriters for magazines do not necessarily specialize in one area of sports, but instead, routinely write features on a wide variety of sports and athletes, sportswriters for newspapers do specialize. Many only cover a particular sport, such as baseball. Others are assigned a beat, or specific area, and like other reporters must cover all the events that fall into that beat. For example, a sportswriter assigned to the high school football beat for a newspaper in Los Angeles, California, would be expected to cover all the area high school football games. Since football is seasonal, he or she might be assigned to the high school basketball beat during the winter season. On the other hand, the sportswriter working in Lexington, Kentucky, might be assigned coverage of all the high school sports in the area, not simply one sport. Much of the way in which assignments are given depends on experience as well as budget and staffing constraints.

REQUIREMENTS

High School

English, journalism, and speech are the most important classes for you to take in high school. You will need to master the art of writing in order to be able to convey your ideas concisely, yet creatively, to your readers. Speech classes will help you become comfortable interacting with others. Be sure to take physical education classes and participate in organized sports, be it as a competitor, a team manager, or an assistant. You also should join the staff of your school newspaper or yearbook. This will give you a chance to cover and write about your school's sports teams or other school activities.

Postsecondary Training

You will need at least a bachelor's degree to become a sportswriter, although many sportswriters go on to study journalism at the graduate level. Most sportswriters concentrate on journalism while in college, either by attending a program in journalism or by taking whatever courses are available outside of a specialized program. This is not to say that you cannot become a sportswriter without a degree in journalism, but competition for sportswriting jobs is incredibly fierce. After all, sportswriters get great seats at sports events, and they have the credentials to get them into interviews with sports celebrities. Increasingly, a specialized education is becoming the means by which sports editors and managers sift through the stacks of resumes from prospective sportswriters. Sportswriters may have degrees in communications or English, among other majors.

Other Requirements

Clearly, the ability to write well and concisely is another requirement for the job of the sportswriter. In addition, you must have a solid understanding of the rules and play of many different sports. If you hope to specialize in the coverage of one particular sport, your knowledge of that sport has to be equal to that of anyone coaching or playing it at the professional level.

Finally, you must be able to elicit information from a variety of sources, as well as to determine when information being leaked is closer to promotional spin than to fact. There will be more times when a coach or agent will not want to comment on a story than the times when they will want to make an on-the-record comment, so the sportswriter must be assertive in pressing the source for more information.

EXPLORING

You can learn on-the-job skills by working for your high school and college newspapers. The experience can be related to sports, of course, but any journalistic experience will help you develop the basic skills useful to any reporter, regardless of the area about which you are writing.

You can increase your chances and success in the field by applying to colleges or universities with renowned academic programs in journalism. Most accredited programs have a required period of training in which you will intern with a major newspaper somewhere in the United States; student-interns are responsible for covering a beat.

You may also find it helpful to read the sports section of your local newspaper or other publications that are related to this field, such as *Sports Illustrated* (http://sportsillustrated.cnn.com) and *Sports Business Journal* (http://www.sportsbusinessjournal.com), and visit Web sites such as the Associated Press Sports Editors (http://apsportseditors.org). You can also read books about sportswriting, including collections of the best sportswriting of the year.

Finally, ask your journalism teacher or counselor to arrange an information interview with a sportswriter.

EMPLOYERS

Sportswriters are employed by newspapers and magazines throughout the world. They may cover professional teams based in large cities or high school teams located in tiny towns. Sportswriters also work as freelance writers.

STARTING OUT

You may have to begin your career as a sportswriter by covering the games or matches that no else wants to or can cover. As a stringer, you will not earn much money, so you will probably have a second or even third job, but eventually it may lead to covering bigger and better games and teams. Some sportswriters make a living out of covering sports for very small towns, others only work at those jobs until they have gained the experience to move on.

Most journalists start their careers by working in small markets—little towns and cities with local papers. You may work for a newspaper for a year or two and then apply for positions with larger papers in bigger towns and cities. Sportswriters for newspapers follow the same routine, and more than a few end up pursuing areas other than sports because the job openings in sports simply were not there. The lucky few who hang on to a small sports beat can often parlay that beat into a better position by sticking with the job and demonstrating a devotion to the sport, even cultivating a following of loyal fans. This could lead to a full-time column.

Most likely, as a sportswriter, you will take advantage of opportunities to learn more about athletes and sports in general. Becoming an expert on a little known but rapidly growing sport may be one way for you to do this. For example, if you were to learn all that you can about mountain biking, you might be able to land a job with one of the magazines specializing in the sport of mountain biking.

Competition for full-time jobs with magazines as a sportswriter is just as keen as it is for major newspapers. Often, a sportswriter will write articles and try to sell them to one of the major magazines, hoping that when an opening comes, he or she will have first crack at it. Still, most sportswriters move into the world of sports magazines after they have proven themselves in newspaper sportswriting. It is possible, however, to get a job with a sports magazine straight from college or graduate school; you will probably have to work your way up, though.

The career services offices of colleges or universities with accredited undergraduate and graduate programs in journalism can be extremely helpful in beginning your job search. In fact, many graduates of these programs are not only highly sought after by newspapers and magazines, but these graduates are often offered jobs by the newspapers and magazines with which they had an internship during school.

ADVANCEMENT

The constraints of budget, staffing, and time—which make a sportswriter's job difficult—are also often what can help a sportswriter rise through the ranks. For example, the writer asked to cover all the sports in a small area may have to hustle to cover the beat alone, but that writer also will not have any competition when covering the big events. Thus, he or she can gain valuable experience and bylines writing for a small paper, whereas in a larger market, the same sportswriter would have to wait much longer to be assigned an event that might result in a coveted byline.

Sportswriters advance by gaining the top assignments, covering the major sports in feature articles, as opposed to the bare-bones summaries of events. They also advance by moving to larger and larger papers, by getting columns, and finally, by getting a syndicated column—that is, a column carried by many papers around the country or even around the world.

Sportswriters for magazines advance by moving up the publishing ladder, from editorial assistant to associate editor to writer. Often, an editorial assistant might be assigned to research a story for a sports brief—a quirky or short look at an element of the game. For example, *Sports Illustrated* might have a page devoted to new advances in sports equipment for the amateur athlete. The editorial assistant might be given the idea and asked to research it, or specific items. A writer might eventually write it up, using the editorial assistant's notes. Advancement, then, comes in being actually listed as the author of the piece.

In the publishing worlds of both newspapers and magazines, sportswriters can advance by becoming editors of a newspaper's sports page or of a sports magazine. There are also sports publicists and sports information directors who work for the publicity and promotions arms of colleges, universities, and professional sports teams. These individuals release statements, write and disseminate to the press articles on the organizations' teams and athletes, and arrange press opportunities for coaches and athletes.

EARNINGS

According the U.S. Department of Labor, writers earned median annual salaries of $53,900 in 2009. The lowest paid 10 percent earned less than $28,070, while the highest paid 10 percent earned $105,710 or more. Mean annual earnings for writers employed by newspaper, periodical, book, and directory publishers were $53,050 in 2009. Those who worked in radio and television broadcasting earned $65,330.

Sportswriters who cover the major sports events, who have their own column, or who have a syndicated column can expect to earn more than the salaries above. Sportswriters who write for major magazines can also expect to earn more, sometimes per article, depending on their reputations and the contracts worked out by themselves or their agents.

Benefits for full-time staff writers include vacation and sick time, health, and sometimes dental, insurance, and pension or 401(k) plans. Self-employed writers must provide their own benefits.

WORK ENVIRONMENT

Like other journalists, sportswriters work in a variety of conditions, from the air-conditioned offices of a newsroom or magazine publisher to the sweaty, humid locker room of a professional basketball team, to the arid and dusty field where a baseball team's spring training is held. Sportswriters work irregular hours, putting in as much or as little time as the story requires, often traveling to small towns and out-of-the-way locales to cover a team's away games.

The benefits are obvious—for the individuals who love sports, the job offers the chance to cover sports events every day; to immerse themselves in the statistics and injury lists and bidding wars of professional and amateur sports; and to speak, sometimes one-on-one, with the greatest athletes of yesterday, today, and tomorrow.

OUTLOOK

The turnover rate for top sportswriters with major newspapers and magazines is not very high, which means that job openings occur as sportswriters retire, die, are fired, or move into other markets. While the publishing industry may have room in it for yet another magazine devoted to a particular sports specialty, competition for sportswriting jobs will continue to be strong through 2018 and beyond.

FOR MORE INFORMATION

This is the official Web site of the Associated Press Sports Editors, a membership organization that strives to improve print journalistic standards in sports newsrooms. Visit its Web site to find up-to-date news articles regarding industry happenings, a job board, and a downloadable monthly newsletter, as well as links to all of the major professional sports organizations and leagues.

Associated Press Sports Editors
http://apsportseditors.org

This organization provides general educational information on all areas of journalism, including newspapers, magazines, television, Internet, and radio. Members include journalism and mass communication faculty, administrators, students, and media professionals.

Association for Education in Journalism and Mass Communication
234 Outlet Pointe Boulevard, Suite A
Columbia, SC 29210-5667
Tel: 803-798-0271
E-mail: aejmchq@aol.com
http://www.aejmc.com

The AWSM is a membership organization of women and men employed in sports writing, editing, broadcast and production, public relations, and sports information. Visit its Web site for information on internships and scholarships.

Association for Women in Sports Media (AWSM)
3899 North Front Street
Harrisburg, PA 17110-1583
Tel: 717-703-3086
http://awsmonline.org

To learn more about baseball writers, visit
Baseball Writers' Association of America
E-mail: info@bbwaa.com
http://bbwaa.com

Visit the fund's Web site for information on print and online journalism careers, college and university journalism programs, high school journalism workshops, scholarships, internships, and job listings.

Dow Jones News Fund
PO Box 300
Princeton, NJ 08543-0300
Tel: 609-452-2820
E-mail: djnf@dowjones.com
https://www.newsfund.org

For information on careers, contact
Football Writers Association of America
http://www.sportswriters.net/fwaa

Visit the society's Web site for information on membership and scholarships for college students and to read The Columnist *newsletter.*

National Society of Newspaper Columnists
PO Box 411532
San Francisco, CA 94141-1532
Tel: 415-488-6762
http://www.columnists.com

For information on writers who cover horse racing, contact
National Turf Writers Association
E-mail: info@turfwriters.org
http://www.turfwriters.org

This is a trade union for "freelance and contract writers: journalists, book authors, business and technical writers, Web content providers, and poets." Visit its Web site for resources for journalists and writers.

National Writers Union
256 West 38th Street, Suite 703
New York, NY 10018-9807
Tel: 212-254-0279
E-mail: nwu@nwu.org
http://www.nwu.org

The nonprofit organization represents the $47 billion newspaper industry and more than 2,000 newspapers in the United States and Canada. Visit its Web site for information on trends in the industry and careers (including digital media job descriptions).

Newspaper Association of America
4401 Wilson Boulevard, Suite 900
Arlington, VA 22203-1867
Tel: 571-366-1000
http://www.naa.org

The guild is a union for journalists, advertising sales workers, and other media professionals.

The Newspaper Guild-Communications Workers of America
501 Third Street, NW, 6th Floor
Washington, DC 20001-2797
Tel: 202-434-7177
E-mail: guild@cwa-union.org
http://www.newsguild.org

Visit the society's Web site for information on student chapters and scholarships for college students, job listings, training opportunities, educational resources, discussion boards and blogs, and much more.

Society of Professional Journalists
3909 North Meridian Street
Indianapolis, IN 46208-4011
Tel: 317-927-8000
http://www.spj.org

Visit the following Web site for comprehensive information on journalism careers, summer programs, and college journalism programs:

High School Journalism
http://www.hsj.org

INTERVIEW

Ed West is a sportswriter at the Billings Gazette *in Billings, Montana. He has been a sportswriter for more than 35 years. Ed discussed his career with the editors of* Careers in Focus: Journalism.

Q. When did you decide to become a sportswriter?

A. I was in college and thinking about a teaching career. I wasn't sure if that's what I really wanted to do, however, and a friend of mine suggested I try to get a part-time job in the sports department at the *Gazette*. He'd worked at the *Gazette* and said they usually needed five or six part-timers every sports season. I was hired and ended up really enjoying it.

Q. Take us through a day in your life as a sportswriter. What are your typical tasks/responsibilities?

A. My main responsibility is coverage of our four local high schools. My beat includes football, boys' basketball, soccer, and track. I also receive assignments for volleyball, girls' basketball, and softball.

We also have two local colleges, and I'll occasionally get an assignment to cover one of their teams, primarily in basketball.

We do not have high school baseball here, but there is a strong American Legion program, which is my beat in the summer. I will cover some games of our professional team, the Billings Mustangs.

My beat includes writing game stories and features. I also try to write a weekly column. I generally work Tuesdays through Saturdays. I usually arrive at the office around 12:30 to 1 P.M. and try to get started on whatever assignment I have (usually a column or feature story). I try to contact coaches in the late afternoon or in the evening if I can't get them before practice.

I'm usually involved with game coverage on Friday and Saturday nights in the fall and quite a few days of the week in the winter. In the spring, most track meets are in the morning and afternoon. Summer coverage generally involves a lot of night baseball games.

Q. What do you like most and least about your job?

A. I enjoy covering the games and have met a lot of new people. Our sports staff through the years has always been a pleasure to work with. It can get tense sometimes on deadline, but the people here have been able to work well together with a sense of humor.

The biggest downside is probably the fact that some fans believe we favor one school over another.

Q. What advice would you give to high school students who are interested in becoming sportswriters?

A. If a student has an interest in a career in the media, I would suggest getting involved with the school newspaper. Your local paper may have part-time positions that can help you decide about a potential career in the business. While I did not get a journalism/communications degree, I would recommend that whether you're interested in newspapers, radio, television, or another electronic medium.

Writers

QUICK FACTS

School Subjects
English
Journalism

Personal Skills
Communication/ideas
Helping/teaching

Work Environment
Primarily indoors
Primarily one location

Minimum Education Level
Bachelor's degree

Salary Range
$28,070 to $53,900 to
$105,710+

Certification or Licensing
None available

Outlook
Faster than the average

DOT
131

GOE
01.02.01

NOC
5121

O*NET-SOC
27-3043.00

OVERVIEW

Journalistic *writers* express, edit, promote, and interpret ideas and facts in written form for newspapers, magazines, books, Web sites, and radio and television broadcasts. There are approximately 151,700 salaried writers in the United States.

HISTORY

The skill of writing has existed for thousands of years. Papyrus fragments with writing by ancient Egyptians date from about 3000 B.C., and archaeological findings show that the Chinese had developed books by about 1300 B.C. A number of technical obstacles had to be overcome before printing and the profession of writing evolved. Books of the Middle Ages were copied by hand on parchment. The ornate style that marked these books helped ensure their rarity. Also, few people were able to read. Religious fervor prohibited the reproduction of secular literature.

The development of the printing press by Johannes Gutenberg in the middle of the 15th century and the liberalism of the Protestant Reformation, which helped encourage a wider range of publications, greater literacy, and the creation of a number of works of literary merit, helped develop the publishing industry. The first authors worked directly with printers.

The modern publishing age began in the 18th century. Printing became mechanized, and the novel, magazine, and newspaper developed. The first newspaper in the American colonies appeared in the early 18th century, but it was Benjamin Franklin who, as editor and writer, made the *Pennsylvania Gazette* one of the most influential in setting a high standard for his fellow American journalists. Franklin

Nellie Bly (1864–1922)

Elizabeth Jane Cochrane is considered one of the pioneers of investigative reporting. If this name does not ring a bell, perhaps her pseudonym will—Nellie Bly.

Female reporters were a rarity during the 1880s and the few who did work in the industry were often assigned to cover fashion, gardening, or society. However, Bly was not interested in writing about any of those topics; she used her investigative and writing skills to uncover many of society's ills. Bly often went "undercover" to research a topic. She once lived in Mexico when reporting on the country's suppression at the hands of its dictator. For a report on the mistreatment of the mentally ill, Bly had herself committed to an insane asylum in New York. Her investigative piece on the asylum resulted in a major reorganization of the Women's Lunatic Asylum at Blackwell Island, and increased funding from the Department of Public Charities and Corrections.

Her life and work has been the subject of books, plays, video game characters, and an amusement park. In 2002, the United States Post Office honored Nellie Bly with a commemorative postage stamp as part of the "Women in Journalism" postage set.

Sources: Nelliebly.org, National Women's Hall of Fame

---

also published the first magazine in the colonies, *The American Magazine*, in 1741.

Advances in the printing trades, photoengraving, retailing, and the availability of capital produced a boom in newspapers and magazines in the 19th century. Further mechanization in the printing field, such as the use of the Linotype machine, high-speed rotary presses, and special color reproduction processes, set the stage for still further growth in the book, newspaper, and magazine industry.

In addition to the print media, the broadcasting industry has contributed to the development of the professional writer. Radio, television, and the Internet are sources of information, education, and entertainment that provide employment for thousands of journalistic writers.

THE JOB

Journalistic writers deal with the written word, whether it is destined for the printed page, broadcast, or computer screen. The nature of their work is as varied as the materials they produce: newspapers, magazines, books, content for Web sites, and scripts for radio and television broadcast. Writers develop ideas and write for all media.

Staff writers are employed by magazines and newspapers to write news stories, feature articles, and columns about a wide variety of subjects, including politics, government, education, entertainment, sports, science, health, food, consumer affairs, and local, regional, or national news. First they come up with an idea for an article from their own interests or are assigned a topic by an editor. The topic is of relevance to the particular publication; for example, a writer for a magazine on entertainment may be assigned an article on the Academy Awards. Then writers begin gathering as much information as possible about the subject through library research, interviews, the Internet, observation, and other methods. They keep extensive notes from which they will draw material for their project. Once the material has been organized and arranged in logical sequence, writers prepare a written outline. The process of developing a piece of writing is exciting, although it can also involve detailed and solitary work. After researching an idea, a writer might discover that a different perspective or related topic would be more effective, entertaining, or marketable.

Columnists or *commentators* analyze news and social issues. They write about events from the standpoint of their own experience or opinion.

Editorial writers write on topics of public interest, and their comments, consistent with the viewpoints and policies of their employers, are intended to stimulate or mold public opinion.

Foreign correspondents report on news from countries outside of where their newspapers or magazines are located. Other foreign correspondents work for radio or television networks.

Critics review restaurants, books, works of art, movies, plays, musical performances, and other cultural events.

Newswriters work for radio or TV news departments writing news stories, news "teases," special features, investigative reports, and entire newscasts, which include news, weather, sports, traffic reports, and other broadcast content. They do this by researching and fact-checking information obtained from reporters, newswires, press releases, research, and telephone and e-mail interviews. Newswriters must be able to write clear, concise stories that fit in a specific allotted time period. Newswriters employed in television broadcasting must be able to match the words they write with the images that are broadcast to help illustrate the story. Since most radio and television stations broadcast 24 hours a day, newswriters are needed to work daytime, evening, and overnight shifts.

When working on assignment, writers usually submit their outlines to an editor or other company representative for approval. Then they write a first draft, trying to put the material into words that will have the desired effect on their audience. They often rewrite or polish sections of the material as they proceed, always searching for just the right way of imparting information or expressing an idea or opinion. A manuscript may be reviewed, corrected, and revised numerous times before a final copy is submitted. Even after that, an editor may request additional changes.

Writers for newspapers, magazines, or books often specialize in their subject matter. Some writers might have an educational background that allows them to give critical interpretations or analyses. For example, a health or science writer for a newspaper typically has a degree in biology and can interpret new ideas in the field for the average reader.

Writers can be employed either as in-house staff or as freelancers. Pay varies according to experience and the position, but freelancers must provide their own office space and equipment such as computers and fax machines. Freelancers also are responsible for keeping tax records, sending out invoices, negotiating contracts, and providing their own health insurance.

REQUIREMENTS

High School
While in high school, build a broad educational foundation by taking courses in English, literature, foreign languages, history, general science, social studies, computer science, and typing. The ability to type is almost a requisite for many positions in the journalism field, as is familiarity with computers.

Postsecondary Training
Competition for journalistic writing jobs almost always demands the background of a college education. Many employers prefer you to have a broad liberal arts background or majors in English, literature, history, philosophy, or one of the social sciences. Other employers desire communications or journalism training in college. Occasionally a master's degree in a specialized writing field may be required. A number of schools offer courses in journalism, and some of them offer courses or majors in newspaper and magazine writing, publication management, book publishing, and writing for the Internet.

Visit the Web site of the Accrediting Council on Education in Journalism and Mass Communications (http://www2.ku.edu/~acejmc/STUDENT/PROGLIST.SHTML) for a list of accredited postsecondary training programs in journalism and mass communications.

In addition to formal course work, most employers look for practical writing experience. If you have worked on high school or college newspapers, yearbooks, or literary magazines, you will make a better candidate, as well as if you have worked for small community newspapers or radio stations, even in an unpaid position. Many magazines, newspapers, and radio and television stations have summer internship programs that provide valuable training if you want to learn about the publishing and broadcasting businesses. Interns do many simple tasks, such as running errands and answering phones, but some may be asked to perform research, conduct interviews, or even write some minor pieces.

Other Requirements
To be a journalistic writer, you should be creative and able to express ideas clearly, have a broad general knowledge, be skilled in research techniques, and be computer literate. Other assets include curiosity, persistence, initiative, resourcefulness, and an accurate memory. For some jobs—on a newspaper or a television newsroom, for example, where the activity is hectic and deadlines are short—the ability to concentrate and produce under pressure is essential.

EXPLORING

As a high school or college student, you can test your interest and aptitude in the field of writing by serving as a reporter or writer on school newspapers, yearbooks, and literary magazines. Various writing courses and workshops will offer you the opportunity to sharpen your writing skills.

Small community newspapers and local radio stations often welcome contributions from outside sources, although they may not have the resources to pay for them. Jobs in bookstores, magazine shops, and even newsstands will offer you a chance to become familiar with various publications.

You can also obtain information on writing as a career by visiting local newspapers, publishers, or radio and television stations and interviewing some of the writers who work there. Career conferences and other guidance programs frequently include speakers on the entire field of journalism from local or national organizations.

EMPLOYERS

There are approximately 151,700 writers and authors in the United States. Many writers work for newspapers, magazines, and book publishers; radio and television broadcasting companies; and Internet publishing and broadcasting companies. Outside the field of journalism, writers are also employed by advertising agencies, public relations firms, and for journals and newsletters published by business and nonprofit organizations, such as professional associations, labor unions, and religious organizations. Other non-journalism employers are government agencies and film production companies. Other writers work as novelists, short story writers, poets, playwrights, and screenwriters.

The major newspaper, magazine, and book publishers and broadcasting companies account for the concentration of journalistic writers in large cities such as New York, Chicago, Los Angeles, Boston, Philadelphia, San Francisco, and Washington, D.C. Opportunities with small publishers and broadcasting companies can be found throughout the country.

STARTING OUT

A fair amount of experience is required to gain a high-level position in the field. Most writers start out in entry-level positions. These jobs may be listed with college career services offices, or they may be obtained by applying directly to the employment departments of the individual publishers or broadcasting companies. Graduates who previously served internships with these companies often have the advantage of knowing someone who can give them a personal recommendation. Want ads in newspapers and trade journals are another source for jobs. Because of the competition for positions, however, few vacancies are listed with public or private employment agencies.

Employers in the field of journalism usually are interested in samples of published writing. These are often assembled in an organized portfolio or scrapbook. Bylined or signed articles are more credible (and, as a result, more useful) than stories whose source is not identified.

Beginning positions as a junior writer usually involve library research, preparation of rough drafts for part or all of a report, cataloging, and other related writing tasks. These are generally carried on under the supervision of a senior writer.

ADVANCEMENT

Most writers find their first jobs as editorial, production, or research assistants. Advancement may be more rapid in small media companies, where beginners learn by doing a little bit of everything and may be given writing tasks immediately. At large publishers or broadcast companies, duties are usually more compartmentalized. Assistants in entry-level positions are assigned such tasks as research and fact checking, but it generally takes much longer to advance to full-scale writing duties.

Promotion into higher positions may come with the assignment of more important articles and stories to write, or it may be the result of moving to another company. Mobility among employees in this field is common. A staff writer at one magazine publisher may switch to a similar position at a more prestigious publication. Or a newswriter may switch to a related field as a type of advancement.

Freelance or self-employed writers earn advancement in the form of larger fees as they gain exposure and establish their reputations.

EARNINGS

In 2009, median earnings for all salaried writers were $53,900 a year, according to the U.S. Department of Labor (DOL). The lowest paid 10 percent earned less than $28,070, while the highest paid 10 percent earned $105,710 or more. Writers employed by newspaper and book publishers had annual mean earnings of $53,050, while those employed in radio and television broadcasting earned $65,330.

In addition to their salaries, many writers earn some income from freelance work. Part-time freelancers may earn from $5,000 to $15,000 a year. Freelance earnings vary widely. Full-time, established freelance writers may earn $75,000 or more a year.

Benefits for full-time staff writers include vacation and sick time, health, and sometimes dental, insurance, and pension or 401(k) plans. Self-employed writers must provide their own benefits.

WORK ENVIRONMENT

Working conditions vary for journalistic writers. Although their workweek usually runs 35 to 40 hours, many writers work overtime. A publication that is issued frequently has more deadlines closer together, creating greater pressures to meet them. The work is especially hectic on newspapers and at broadcasting companies that operate seven days a week. Writers often work nights and weekends to meet deadlines or to cover a late-developing story.

Most writers work independently, but they often must cooperate with editors, artists, photographers, and rewriters who may have widely differing ideas of how the materials should be prepared and presented.

Physical surroundings range from comfortable private offices to noisy, crowded newsrooms filled with other workers typing and talking on the telephone. Some writers must confine their research to the library or telephone interviews, but others may travel to other cities or countries or to local sites, such as theaters, ballparks, airports, factories, or other offices.

The work is arduous, but most writers are seldom bored. Some jobs, such as that of the foreign correspondent, require travel. The most difficult element is the continual pressure of deadlines. People who are the most content as writers enjoy and work well under deadline pressure.

OUTLOOK

The employment of all writers is expected to increase faster than the average for all occupations through 2018, according to the DOL. The demand for writers by newspapers, periodicals, and book publishers is expected to increase—although publications that are funded by advertising revenue and sales receipts will offer fewer opportunities for writers. The growth of electronic publishing will also demand many talented writers; those with computer skills will be at an advantage as a result. Employment for all positions in the radio and television broadcasting industry is expected to increase by 7 percent, more slowly than the average for all industries through 2018, according to the DOL.

People entering this field should realize that the competition for jobs is extremely keen. Beginners, especially, may have difficulty finding employment. Of the thousands who graduate each year with degrees in English, journalism, communications, and the liberal arts intending to establish a career as a writer, many turn to other occupations when they find that applicants far outnumber the job openings available. College students would do well to keep this in mind and prepare for an unrelated alternate career in the event they are unable to obtain a position as writer; another benefit of this approach is that, at the same time, they will become qualified as writers in a specialized field. The practicality of preparing for alternate careers is borne out by the fact that opportunities are best in firms that prepare business and trade publications and in technical writing.

Potential writers who end up working in a field other than journalism may be able to earn some income as freelancers, selling articles, stories, books, and possibly TV and movie scripts, but it is usually difficult for anyone to be self-supporting entirely on independent writing.

FOR MORE INFORMATION

The ACEJMC is "responsible for the evaluation of professional journalism and mass communications programs in colleges and universities." Visit its Web site for a list of accredited programs.
Accrediting Council on Education in Journalism and
    Mass Communications (ACEJMC)
University of Kansas School of Journalism and
    Mass Communications
Stauffer-Flint Hall, 1435 Jayhawk Boulevard
Lawrence, KS 66045-7575
Tel: 785-864-3973
http://www2.ku.edu/~acejmc/STUDENT/PROGLIST.SHTML

The society provides information on careers in reporting, as well as details on education and financial aid (from outside sources).
American Society of Journalists and Authors
1501 Broadway, Suite 302
New York, NY 10036-5505
Tel: 212-997-0947
http://www.asja.org

This organization provides general educational information on all areas of journalism, including newspapers, magazines, television, Internet, and radio. Members include journalism and mass communication faculty, administrators, students, and media professionals.
Association for Education in Journalism and
    Mass Communication
234 Outlet Pointe Boulevard, Suite A
Columbia, SC 29210-5667
Tel: 803-798-0271
E-mail: aejmchq@aol.com
http://www.aejmc.com

*An association of university broadcasting faculty, industry profes-
sionals, and graduate students, BEA offers annual scholarships in
broadcasting for college juniors, seniors, and graduate students.
Visit its Web site for useful information about broadcast education
and the broadcasting industry.*

Broadcast Education Association
1771 N Street, NW
Washington, DC 20036-2891
Tel: 202-429-3935
http://www.beaweb.org

*Visit the fund's Web site for information on print and online jour-
nalism careers, college and university journalism programs, high
school journalism workshops, scholarships, internships, and job
listings.*

Dow Jones News Fund
PO Box 300
Princeton, NJ 08543-0300
Tel: 609-452-2820
E-mail: djnf@dowjones.com
https://www.newsfund.org

*The EFA is an organization for freelance writers, editors, and other
publishing professionals. Members receive a newsletter and a free
listing in its directory.*

Editorial Freelancers Association (EFA)
71 West 23rd Street, 4th Floor
New York, NY 10010-4102
Tel: 212-929-5400
E-mail: office@the-efa.org
http://www.the-efa.org

*This is a membership organization for science writers employed
in all areas of journalism. Visit its Web site for information on
careers in science writing and membership and internships for college students.*

National Association of Science Writers
PO Box 7905
Berkeley, CA 94707-0905
Tel: 510-647-9500
http://www.nasw.org

Visit the conference's Web site for information on membership and scholarships for college students and answers to frequently asked questions about a career as an editorial writer.
National Conference of Editorial Writers
3899 North Front Street
Harrisburg, PA 17110-1583
Tel: 717-703-3015
E-mail: ncew@pa-news.org
http://www.ncew.org

Visit the society's Web site for information on membership and scholarships for college students and to read The Columnist *newsletter.*
National Society of Newspaper Columnists
PO Box 411532
San Francisco, CA 94141-1532
Tel: 415-488-6762
http://www.columnists.com

This is a trade union for "freelance and contract writers: journalists, book authors, business and technical writers, Web content providers, and poets." Visit its Web site for resources for journalists and writers.
National Writers Union
256 West 38th Street, Suite 703
New York, NY 10018-9807
Tel: 212-254-0279
E-mail: nwu@nwu.org
http://www.nwu.org

The guild is a union for journalists, advertising sales workers, and other media professionals.
The Newspaper Guild-Communications Workers of America
501 Third Street, NW, 6th Floor
Washington, DC 20001-2797
Tel: 202-434-7177
E-mail: guild@cwa-union.org
http://www.newsguild.org

Visit this organization's Web site to access scholarship and internship information (for college students), high school journalism resources and programs (such as the High School Broadcast Journalism Project), useful publications, and salary and employment surveys. The association also offers membership to college students.
Radio Television Digital News Association
529 14th Street, NW, Suite 425

Washington, DC 20045-1406
Tel: 202-659-6510
http://www.rtdna.org

Visit the society's Web site for information on student chapters and scholarships for college students, job listings, training opportunities, educational resources, discussion boards and blogs, and much more.
Society of Professional Journalists
3909 North Meridian Street
Indianapolis, IN 46208-4011
Tel: 317-927-8000
http://www.spj.org

Visit the following Web site for comprehensive information on journalism careers, summer programs, and college journalism programs:
High School Journalism
http://www.hsj.org

INTERVIEW

Dan Lybarger is a film critic who has contributed work to the Kansas City Star, Cineaste, *Nitrate Online, the* Lawrence Journal-World, *RottenTomatoes.com,* PitchWeekly, *KCactive.com, and other publications and Web sites. He discussed his career with the editors of* Careers in Focus: Journalism.

Q. What made you want to become a film critic?

A. When I was six years old, my teacher showed the rest of the class and me only half of a Lassie movie. Poor Lassie was stuck in a pit when the lights came up, and I complained about the film, informing the teacher that if the movie were any good, Lassie would get out. Ever since then, I've simply wanted movies to live up to their potential.

Q. How did you get your first job in the field?

A. When I attended the University of Arkansas at Little Rock (UALR), I met up with the executive editor of *Spectrum Weekly* at a bar (what a fine example I set for America's youth!). I told him I wrote reviews for the *UALR Forum*, and he politely asked, "Would you like to write for us." I sent them some samples, and then I contributed to them regularly for a year before I started writing here in Kansas City.

Q. Can you describe a typical day on the job?

A. I have a couple of outlets, but I'm a freelancer, and I have a day job. While I am deeply grateful for the compensation I receive, I could never simply be just a film critic. My editors might assign me to watch a film, or I might volunteer to see it. I would then attend a screening of the film or watch a screener DVD. I then write my review at home. This can take two to three hours to write a 600-word review. Because I write for online outlets as well as print, I might have to write the review immediately after I've seen the movie or I may have a few days or weeks to get my review done.

When I conduct interviews, I usually read as much as I can about the filmmaker I'm interviewing so that I don't ask any obvious or hackneyed questions. Usually I have 20 minutes with the subject. I record the conversation and then listen to the recording and isolate the quotes that are most relevant and then write the piece.

If you like regular hours, don't become a film critic in a mid-level market like Kansas City. Your schedule can vary depending on how many films are screening and if it is a peak season like Christmas or summer.

As for my responsibilities, I have to turn in my review so that my editor or I can post it on opening day. With some releases, early reviews violate agreements with studios. My editors expect me to give both a description of the film and my opinion of it without giving away important plot twists.

Q. What do you like least and most about work as a film critic?

A. I love getting paid, helping people find movies they will adore, discovering amazing films I wouldn't have seen otherwise, learning what makes good movies effective, and the adrenaline rush from trying to meet a deadline.

I hate the unsteadiness of the work (many of my outlets have closed over the years), waiting for checks, sitting through lousy films at full attention, writer's block, and discovering ways I could have expressed myself better if I'd had more time to compose my pieces.

Q. What has been one of the most rewarding or interesting experiences in your career as a film critic?

A. I'm from Kansas City, and Robert Altman was revered here. I once had the privilege of interviewing him for *Gosford Park* and later screened the film with a group of his local relatives. While Altman used to lament that his friends and family in Kansas City didn't get his movies, his relatives here grasped everything in the film and had some really good comments. They loved his overlapping dialogue ("That's just how people talk.") and said that his bluntness in interviews was typical of the family ("We're all like that. Sometimes it's for the best. Sometimes it isn't.").

When Altman died, I had the pleasure of hosting, with the Kansas City Film Critics Circle, a screening of M*A*S*H where we also included one of the industrial films he shot here in Kansas City for the Calvin Company. Some of Altman's former collaborators came to the event, and I had a wonderful Q&A session with them after the movie. It was wonderful to see the films and to let Kansas Citians know that a talent like Altman's didn't just come out of a vacuum.

Q. What is your favorite movie and why?

A. Billy Wilder's *The Apartment*. I think the film is quite touching and also side-splittingly funny. Even though I've seen it dozens of times, I still get choked up at the ending.

As a writer, I am intimidated by the fact that Wilder and I.A.L. Diamond [the screenwriter] both came to this country speaking very little English, and yet their witty dialogue puts the wordplay of most native English speakers to shame.

At the time I discovered the film, I was working in a bureaucratic environment like the one it depicted. As the film progressed, I was struck by how even ordinary people like the Jack Lemmon character had to make decisions that could have profound moral implications. Wilder and Diamond demonstrated that chasing money and selfish goals could be destructive, but magically made their lesson seem more like entertainment instead of a sermon.

Index